ADVANCE PRAISE

"Reading *The Leader's Secret Code* is like dipping into a box of your favourite chocolates. The book contains such a huge range of immensely powerful leadership stories, all supported by robust references and brought to life with glorious sketches, that I turned every single page with anticipation and delight. I felt like every chapter had been written just for me and the appeal never faded as I made my way through the book. An inspiration and a must-have source of leadership insights. A feast!"

Tracey Groves
CEO, Intelligent Ethics,
FT 2018 Champion of Women in Business

"A thoroughly insightful, evidence-based journey through the world of leadership. We all thrive to understand and lead in times of great uncertainty and this excellent guide demonstrates how your beliefs and behaviours drive high performance: how you have to act differently to make a difference. Highly recommend to anybody in leadership roles."

Nazir Afzal OBE
Former Chief Prosecutor and
Chief Executive of Police & Crime Commissioners

"A compelling read of inspiring insights from scientific analysis of successful leaders which can be applied by anyone, whether you lead a global organization or run a local sports club. Incredibly relevant to the dynamic, turbulent and digital world we live in today."

Dilip Mailvaganam
Business Development Director,
Microsoft Services Emerging Solutions Worldwide

"*The Leader's Secret Code* is packed with timely insights, comprehensive frameworks and a series of leaders' portraits to better understand how to lead in a time of uncertainty and rapid change."

Thomas Roulet
Senior Lecturer in Organization Theory at the
Judge Business School, University of Cambridge

"For me, communication is the key differentiator between good and great leaders. This book is a great read in terms of practical advice from experienced and exceptional leaders. It centres on the essential art of communication and how all core leadership skills, behaviours and mindsets rely upon it."

Hugh Hessing
Chief Operating Officer, Aviva UK

"This is a great piece of work based on science and research and is a must-read for any leader who aspires to perform better. What makes it such a compelling read are the 'iconic' leader examples taken from such different worlds; a ballerina, an entrepreneur, a military leader, a social media executive, a CEO and more. Leadership is very situational and *The Leader's Secret Code* can be applied in any scenario."

Shalini Khemka
Founder and CEO, E2E, Deal Maker,
Global Entrepreneur Programme,
Non-Executive Director, UK Export Finance,
and Business Advisory Board Member, Mayor of London

"What sets this leadership book apart from others is that the insights are based on facts and empirical evidence, and I really like the examples of exceptional leaders that bring the data alive. The narrative has helped me personally to self-reflect and make changes and adjustments to my leadership style. I encourage all leaders to explore what could be difference-making for them from this rich toolbox."

Robert Michael
UK Growth Officer, Aon

"Like many leaders in IT, I have developed my leadership skills through trial and error and, to a large extent, this has served me well. This book is a comprehensive yet accessible set of insights that will help people lead more effectively and efficiently and will augment the value of practical experience. We are all having to lead in an ever-changing world that requires new behaviours and skills and this book will help you to achieve your goals faster."

Andrew Mcmanus
CIO, Eversheds Sutherland

"This book is essential reading for anyone involved in developing an organization's leaders – to stimulate thinking on the importance of mindsets, beliefs and behaviours that underpin the approach of outstanding leaders. This book is full of examples to consider and questions to ponder as regards each person's own leadership, in whatever role. Plus, the authors capture all of the information in a useful and pragmatic framework. I highly recommend it."

Maricar Obieta
Global Head of Learning and Leadership Development, Willis Towers Watson

Published by
LID Publishing Limited
The Record Hall, Studio 204,
16-16a Baldwins Gardens,
London EC1N 7RJ, UK

info@lidpublishing.com
www.lidpublishing.com

A member of:

www.businesspublishersroundtable.com

Printed in Latvia by Jelgavas Tipogrāfija
ISBN: 978-1-912555-44-4

Cover and Page design: Caroline Li

IAN MILLS, MARK RIDLEY, BEN LAKER & ADAM PACIFICO

THE
LEADER'S
SECRET
CODE

THE BELIEF SYSTEMS THAT DISTINGUISH WINNERS

MADRID | MEXICO CITY | LONDON
NEW YORK | BUENOS AIRES
BOGOTA | SHANGHAI | NEW DELHI

CONTENTS

ACKNOWLEDGMENTS
1

FOREWORD
2

CHAPTER ONE
Discovering the Leader's Secret Code
4

CHAPTER TWO
The Iconics
34

CHAPTER THREE
Control
100

CHAPTER FOUR
Resilience
142

CHAPTER FIVE
Influence
170

CHAPTER SIX
Communication
196

CHAPTER SEVEN
Strategy
216

CHAPTER EIGHT
Empowerment
246

CHAPTER NINE
Fulfilment
270

CHAPTER TEN
Unlocking Your Code
294

THE CODE BREAKERS
308

BIBLIOGRAPHY
314

ENDNOTES
325

ACKNOWLEDGMENTS

The authors would like to thank the following for their unerring support throughout the research and writing of this book:

- The entire team at Transform Performance International – the 'engine room' and the source of collaborative creativity
- Brian Doyle, for his invaluable insight and input during the editing process
- All the 'iconic' leaders who have given freely of their time to offer their personal leadership insights
- Duke Corporate Education
- Kevin O'Leary, CEO Red Leadership
- Dirk Teuwen, VP Corporate Societal Responsibility, UCB
- Dr David Pendleton, Professor in Leadership at Henley Business School and Associate Fellow, Said Business School, Oxford University for his insightful contribution to Chapter 1
- Our publishers, LID, for their continued support
- Our families, friends and clients who encouraged us every step of the way.

FOREWORD

When I first read *The Leader's Secret Code* it immediately felt like one of the most relevant books of the year. In a world where the assumptions under which our predecessors led no longer ring true, modern leaders are struggling to find their identities and effective leadership models. Recognizing that the world in which we currently lead is more ambiguous and chaotic than it ever has been, *The Leader's Secret Code* offers its readers a practical guide to analysing and unlocking effective leadership strengths in such a world.

We all want to become better leaders, but this task can feel daunting and intangible. (Even agreeing on a definition of leadership can be a challenge!) This book demystifies leadership broadly and its building blocks specifically. By grounding their claims in psychometric data, our authors have defined and expounded upon the qualities common to successful leaders. These qualities include character traits like resilience and the ability to empower others. *Secret Code* is focused on the process – the launching – of our best selves.

Unique to this book is its emphasis on the motivations of different leadership styles. Not only do the authors identify objective qualities that yield successful leaders, but they also identify our 'Journey Motivators': the beliefs that motivate our actions. These motivators, which so often go unnoticed if we aren't self-aware, remind me that everything we do as leaders is ultimately a reflection of ourselves, an expression of who we are. This book helps us to notice our own inclinations so that we can grow into the leaders we were meant to be.

This book applies across so many different situations. Any leader – from small-business managers to corporate executives – can learn from the guidance of the authors. One of the most critical parts of my own leadership philosophy involves collaboration – successful leadership is a relational endeavour. In this spirit, this book journeys with its readers as an imaginative and innovative conversation partner. It can help you to name concepts about leadership you might have known intuitively, but do not yet have the comprehensive research to help name, frame and utilize. Indeed, among the many strengths of this book are its succinct prose and incisive, data-backed insights. Everyone needs to understand the history of their leadership tendencies and the psychological facets of their leadership profile. This book will help you uncover both.

Change is constant and the new ways in which we are interconnected means that leading others effectively looks different from how it looked before. We have to relate to and connect with a more diverse and broader group of people. *Secret Code* helps us to first know ourselves so that we can be the best leaders we can for others. Successful leadership isn't a secret anymore!

Sanyin Siang
CEO Coach, Author of *The Launch Book* and
Executive Director of Duke University's
Coach K Center on Leadership & Ethics

CHAPTER ONE

DISCOVERING THE LEADER'S SECRET CODE

The release of *The Salesperson's Secret Code*[1] in 2017 led Transform Performance International onto the global stage – keynotes, international press and television, academic meetings and boardrooms. One of the most rigorous evaluations of the behaviour and motivation of top-performing salespeople, *The Salesperson's Secret Code*[2] uncovered a causal chain behind consistent and high-level success, providing evidence that what you believe directly influences how you behave and whether you win or lose. Our 'top-performing' belief system is now being explored and utilized by salespeople in a wide array of industries worldwide.

From our perspective – and our clients echo this – the realization that simply believing something could have as significant an impact on performance as skills, aptitude and experience do is a gift to everyone who strives to perform at their best. And what we uncovered in researching and writing that first book left us wondering about its broader applicability.

Since its publication, we have spent many hours in consultation with global corporations. It was in these meetings, where some very smart and talented people debated, dissected and analysed *The Salesperson's Secret Code*,[3] that we found ourselves asking whether the underlying lesson – that a set of beliefs brings about the best performance – might apply to more than just sales. "Could I become a better leader?" one senior executive asked.

It was this question and our desire to answer it that led us to realise it was time to embark on the next stage of this journey of discovery.

And so we, as part of the global educator network of Duke Corporate Education (Duke CE), a leading provider of customised education consistently ranked in the top three by the *Financial Times*, undertook a collective journey to explore this question.

You now hold in your hands the results of that research and the conclusive answers to the question: how do we unlock *The Leader's Secret Code*?

WHAT IS LEADERSHIP?

Are leaders born or made? Of course, the answer is probably a bit of both. Leaders are born, but they are also made and they use a variety of strategies, tools and techniques to grow, evolve and further their cause. Some people are blessed with the talent to touch hearts and minds and to set others marching to the beat of their leadership drum. They are born with an innate capacity to describe a vision and inspire others to want to be a part of the same shared future. Other people may not have these inherent talents, but they are capable of learning. They're able to model excellence in others, learn from their experiences and adapt.

Most current approaches to leadership have their origins in the 19th or 20th centuries, when the world was a very different place. The Spanish, Napoleonic, Holy Roman, Ottoman and Mughal empires gave way to expansive British, Russian and French empires. World wars, decolonization, the Great Depression and the dawn of the nuclear age all left their mark, and the US rose at a formidable rate, emerging as the new world leader. As the political landscape underwent a series of wrenching transformations, so did the world economy, through the Industrial Revolution, the collapse of Communism and the relentless march of globalization. And, of course, the latter half of the 20th century brought a technological revolution that fundamentally transformed business, organizations and society as a whole.

Millennials – and the Generation Z which followed – are voracious digital consumers. Many of them have literally never experienced a world without connectivity or mobile devices. Yes, there are still areas of our planet that are not wired and cabled, but for those of us living in developed countries it's hard to remember life before Google, Amazon, Apple, Facebook or Instagram. The internet is still relatively young (it celebrated its 30th birthday in March 2019) and yet its pervasive connectivity and reach have had a monumental impact on our lives. It all started with a cable plugged into the phone line and the annoying screech of a modem, and now we possess the entire world in the palm of our hand, inside a small box called the smartphone.

According to the latest Kleiner Perkins *Internet Trends Report*,[4] in 2018 the number of internet users surpassed half the world's population – a mind-boggling 3.6 billion people. When markets reach the mainstream, new growth gets harder to find, as evinced by 0% new smartphone unit shipment growth in 2017. What comes next? How in the world can we manage to keep up with it all?

What is true for people is in many cases even more true for organizations. The way you do business today is completely different from the conventions and best practices taken for granted only a decade ago. (Remember when hoarding knowledge in an organizational silo made one a go-to power broker?) All certainties have now suddenly disappeared, washed away by a stream of connectivity. The internet comes with its share of risks, but it has also provided huge opportunities for those able to unlock the power of emerging technologies. Be it global organizations seeking competitive advantage, organized crime exploiting everyday vulnerabilities or law enforcement pleading for the legislature for funding to keep up with developments, what is obvious is that change is now the new constant.

Jack Welch, the American businessman and former General Electric CEO, is often quoted as saying, "If the rate of change on the outside exceeds the rate of change on the inside, the end is near."

The years pass by, but the rules of competition remain the same: you succeed only if you can understand what is going on, adapt to the evolution of technology and behaviours, and meet the unprecedented demands of new customers. If business and technology go hand-in-hand, the same can be said of the customer experience.

Chris Newitt, Global Performance & Steering Director for Jaguar Land Rover, put it this way: "Why don't we go ahead and spend time with a number of people and find out what they think the future will look like, for their industry and for their business? And then we can apply that, because if we understand what the check-in process of hotels will look like in five years' time, and we adapt that to booking your car in for service, we don't need to look at what Audi, BMW and Mercedes are doing."

Being customer-oriented is everything, Chris told us, but he acknowledged that the automotive industry is never going to be the benchmark of customer service. "And that's because of the frequency of interaction. It's just not frequent enough for people to document it as a benchmark. I need to stay in touch with people who are providing things in different industries. And so, for example, I've spent a few days with people from Marks and Spencer and with [hotelier and philanthropist] Gordon Campbell Gray, looking to understand their approach and adapt it for us."

Added into this is the fact that the world economic order is changing and with it the balance of economic power. Whereas in 2003 China had just 43 companies in the Global 2000, in *Forbes*' 2018 listing there were 291.[5] In the 1980s, the US military coined the acronym 'VUCA' to characterize the *volatility*, *uncertainty*, *complexity* and *ambiguity* of the shifting context in which it was operating. The term seemed so broadly applicable that it was adopted by organizations far and wide – and you'll see us use it repeatedly in these pages. Yet, the term might have been applied at almost any time in the 20th century. Was the era of the First World War or the Great Depression of the 1930s any less uncertain than things seem now? Was the world after the Second World War any less complex?

THE SPEED OF EXPONENTIAL CHANGE

The real difference in the 21st century is speed. Changes happen at a bewildering pace, and accumulate and multiply, driving new developments exponentially. The current era has even been dubbed 'The Exponential Age' by Dean Van Leeuwen of the leadership consultancy Tomorrow Today Global.

But in order to better understand today, we need to begin our examination of leadership with a look back at the 20th century. A content analysis of leadership and management journals from the latter half of the century was conducted by management consultant Richard Pascale[6] and updated by the economist and academic Pankaj Ghemawat.[7] It charts the emergence of each new topic, the extent to which it was researched and written about, and the point at which each fell out of vogue and disappeared from relevant publications. The research demonstrates two points clearly.

First, there was an explosion of interest in these topics as the 20th century drew to a close. This pattern started in earnest around 1980, ten years before the advent of the internet, and it picked up again after 1990, as the internet began to provide access to information on most topics.

Secondly – and much more importantly – the research illustrated that there is no cut-and-dried orthodoxy in leadership: ideas come and go, sometimes spending just a brief time in the sun. But there has been no defining, game-changing viewpoint in the field of leadership. Appropriately enough, Pascale labelled a chart that plotted these trends, 'Business Fads 1950–2000'.[8]

The study did however spotlight one enduring megatrend that gained momentum throughout the 20th century and to this day shows no sign of slowing: the increasing democratization of leadership.[9] Ideas about leadership are at any time a subset of contemporary, dominant ideas in society and this is certainly one of them. Consider the following:

- **Consultation**: At the start of the 20th century, Western societies were rigidly hierarchical and formal and paternalistic. In many developed countries, aristocracy remained firmly entrenched and those with privileged backgrounds and strong connections still took the lion's share of prominent positions in politics, commerce and the professions. This was not a time of equal opportunity or anti-discrimination movements. Women were fighting to be enfranchised; they waited until 1919 in the United Sates and it took almost another decade before voting rights were afforded to women in the UK over the age of 21 in 1928. Enlightened bosses may well have consulted the opinions of those they led, but leaders reserved the right to make the key decisions and often did so with an iron fist.

- **Involvement**: In the middle of the last century, the 'push' factors of authority and hierarchy slowly gave way to more 'pull' factors as the world recovered from the Second World War. It was during this time that the notion of 'vision' became a prominent feature of leadership. Values are always implicit in action, but by mid-century the notions of vision and values appeared more explicitly as a means of attracting and retaining good people in the workplace.

Sony pursued a vision of changing forever the world's perception of Japanese goods being synonymous with poor quality. Walmart's stated purpose was to make it possible for poorer folk to be able to afford what richer people could buy, driving down costs and then prices in the process. In the 1960s, NASA adopted the vision of landing a man on the moon and bringing him back safely to Earth by the end of the decade. These and other organized rallying cries pulled people into a broader purpose, an ambitious vision and the shared values that went with them.

- **Partnership and delegation**: As the century drew to a close, in some parts of the world, democratization accelerated and more people demanded that their views, their voices were heard. There was student unrest in France, the popular uprising (soon quashed) known as the 'Prague Spring' and the civil rights movement, which attracted increasing attention in the United States. People wanted to have authority to make decisions. Against this backdrop, leadership practice was inevitably going to evolve and the era of 'empowerment' and delegation had arrived. It is not that the world moved uniformly from consultation and direction to delegation, but rather that these approaches to leadership became more widely deployed, even shifting the norms of management teams and the expectations of rank and file employees. Wherever in the world you are reading this book, you will know the speed and extent to which this change occurred or is still occurring today.

By the end of the 20th century, there was a widespread notion that each employee had rights and that one of these was the right to be heard. Leadership had to be by consent, and those for whom there was no consent to lead could not do so. That became painfully apparent to Brendan Eich, whose 2014 stint as CEO of the open-source software service Mozilla lasted less than two weeks after the company's employees decided they didn't want to work for him.

Regardless of the leadership approach, however, a key question is whether leadership actually has an appreciable influence on the performance of organizations. There have been several large-scale meta-analyses of the relationship between leadership and the organizational performance.[10] These studies show that leaders do have a consistent impact, but reveal that it's not necessarily huge. Differences in leadership style are thought to account for just 13%–15% of the variance in organizational performance, often related to leaders' influence on such factors as strategy, culture and climate.

A QUESTION OF TIMING

In one of the more recent studies,[11] the authors suggest that a more important question is *when* leadership make its difference. They argue that the difference between good and poor leadership shows up most acutely when times are tough – when opportunities are scarce and the resources required to pursue them are hard to come by, notwithstanding the fact that the seeds of demise are often sown in the good times. The Darwinian takeaway: tough times breed great leaders.

If you look at many of the famous leaders throughout history, you'll notice that they became famous because they navigated through seemingly impossible times. They held the flashlight at the end of the tunnel. Legendary leaders such as Abraham Lincoln, Susan B. Anthony and Franklin Delano Roosevelt come to mind. These prominent historical figures were faced with incredibly complex or catastrophic situations. Instead of cowering in indecision, they reacted boldly and aggressively. Lincoln found himself leading at a time when his country tore itself apart in civil war. Anthony was a leading voice for the cause of social reform and women's suffrage, while Roosevelt guided his country through the Great Depression and into the upheaval of the Second World War. All three, faced with such tumult, threw conventional wisdom out of the window and developed their own playbooks on the spot.

Why was this so?

When people are under stress for sustained periods, predictably bad things happen. They become increasingly wary and tend to interpret each new sign as an indication of more bad things to come. Negative emotions run high and people are more likely to snap at each other and openly display frustration.

They're more prone to being sceptical of the new and different, often rejecting it outright. As the stress continues, fatigue sets in and they become overly pessimistic about the future. Relationships suffer as the focus becomes increasingly insular – one of struggling to stay afloat as a business. And on a personal level, individuals will by now be struggling to stay on an even keel as things deteriorate around them. In fact, there's a high likelihood that the end result will be a complete failure of the business if these stress reactions are not kept in check. Yet, despite the sense of impending doom, not all the changes caused by hard times are bad.

With the right leadership, businesses are more likely to increase their focus on critical components that drive their success. Higher standards and greater demands for efficiency lead companies to get better at assessing performance and refining business processes. The *burning platform*, which is a change management term to describe a situation, an event, a phenomenon that encourages people to take immediate, positive action, creates a motivation for change that in good times may not exist. Things that were tolerated in the good years, that everyone knew were less than optimal, are no longer accepted. In the presence of good leadership, the same pressures that cause people to attack each other can be redirected into greater and more effective teamwork and opportunities for individual growth. For instance, businesses that address challenges effectively will emerge from times of recession stronger than their competition and ready to take advantage of an improved economy.

Based on this belief, we subscribe to the view that leadership is a journey – the process of helping one and all advance toward a destination. And, as you might expect, it all starts with oneself.

An example of this was one of our global manufacturing clients that, like many organizations, had battled the realities of the Financial Crisis. A newly appointed CEO, Hans Henrik Lund, arrived with a mandate for change. He had spent over 25 years on his own personal leadership journey, and the wisdom and insight he'd amassed was to be the catalyst for change. His arrival was an example of how one person would galvanize, inspire, restructure and empower all at the same time. "This isn't about me; it can't be," he said, even though thousands of people looked to him for the answers to all their woes.

This leader understood the power of holding up a mirror to the business, allowing all to see the obvious and brutal truth, in order for them to collectively take the reins of change. The lesson was simple and powerful: it might start with one, but it finishes with many. Leadership is an onerous series of dilemmas that the leader must constantly calibrate. That entails building close relationships yet keeping a suitable distance – actively leading but also blending into the background. At the time of writing, in early 2020, what is certain is that the leader must embrace the unknown. As one executive told us: "If you lead, you must learn ... but above all, you must love the experience."

One of the central tenets of effective leadership is to recognize that you are the role model. You set the tone. If you are positive, confident and optimistic, your people are likely to behave in the same way. If you display focus and determination, they'll be inclined to follow suit. Remember, just as panic and despair are infectious, so are energy and enthusiasm. As you look around your organization, remember the words of Mahatma Gandhi: "Be the change you want to see in the world."

THE LEADER'S SECRET CODE

Our belief is that there is a way for all leaders to become the truly exceptional leaders they aspire to be. To do so, however, requires understanding and skilfully working the levers that unlock the code.

Throughout our extensive research careers, we have found that people generally view their professional and personal lives as an ever-expanding series of learning journeys. Though people might acknowledge the importance of certain beliefs in shaping their mindsets and behaviours, they repeatedly point out that these core beliefs are aspirational, evolving continuously and never finite. We have come to call these core sentiments 'Destination Beliefs'.

To understand how Destination Beliefs are key to high performance, one must first realize that they involve a forward-looking view to the end of a journey. There are many paths to a single destination, and it is, according to our research, the paths you take to your Destination Beliefs – how your Destination Beliefs are synthesized and interpreted – that separate the best from the rest.

JOURNEY MOTIVATORS – FOLLOW THE SIGNPOSTS

We refer to the spectrum of approaches and attitudes that influence your path as 'Journey Motivators'. These send us down particular tracks to our Destination Beliefs, both defining how we respond to what happens to us on the journey and pulling us toward our destination.

At each end of the spectrum for a Destination Belief there is an 'extreme' Journey Motivator. We can say, conclusively, that it is your natural resting place on the spectrum – your precise balance of these Journey Motivators – that defines your optimal performance.

Why? Because, it is not *what* you do, but *why* you do it. For some time now our research and leadership interactions across sectors and geographies have continually highlighted the need for strong personal and organizational purpose. A strong *why* acts as a north star for leading and decision-making in a daunting, constantly changing business environment.

As outlined in *The Salesperson's Secret Code*, the most successful salespeople respond to certain Journey Motivators with greater intensity than they do to others. In turn, these specific responses to the intensity of each Journey Motivator directly influences their behaviour. And resulting behaviours, and thus, Journey Motivator 'profiles', directly correlate to performance.

Simply put, out of 1,000 top salespeople around the globe, the very best all demonstrated precisely the same Journey Motivation balances. One performance tier down, the higher performers all shared the same balance profile. Likewise, lower performers also shared a balance profile. Finally, the same was true for the very lowest performers.

It was concrete proof of the old notion that as you believe, so you will behave. And as you will behave, so you will perform. This in turn reinforced our research and focus on the need for leaders to understand the power of role modelling in everything they do. A former Florida trial lawyer, and personal mentor, who worked for many years with the management teams of international law firms always reminded the partners that the children of those that they lead would know their name; in what context was up to them. Their behaviour as a leader and role model would determine their reputation, their credibility and the respect they had from those around them.

Defining the Destination Beliefs and accompanying pairs of Journey Motivators began with an intensive review of leadership literature – every single article, research paper and academic study we could get our hands on – to guide our thinking, remove bias and increase reliability and applicability to as wide a leadership population as possible.

OUR RESEARCH

The Cross-National Time-Series Data Archive, a library of more than 200 years of annual domestic facts and figures for over 200 countries – and whose 196 categories of information are used by academia, governments, financial entities and media worldwide – was an excellent starting point for looking at leadership trends over time.

Then, through the libraries of numerous universities, we reviewed everything ever written exclusively about leadership (as we wrote this book, totalling 718,802 published items).

In sifting through this mountain of information, using software designed for the task, we noticed the same words cropping up time and again – so often that, as we reviewed the leadership literature, we started to compile a list of them and how frequently they appeared.

The terms most commonly associated with 'leadership' included:

Fulfilment = 150
Compliant = 516
Autocratic = 985
Compassion = 1,354
Courage = 2,431
Resilience = 2,458
Delegation = 2,635
Passion = 3,508
Determination = 3,735
Integrity = 4,622
Dominant = 4,729

Confidence = 9,212
Empowerment = 13,939
Risk = 21,078
Control = 34,428
Influence = 41,039
Values = 53,071
Communication = 54,555
Strategy = 69,899

Glancing through this list, we noticed that some terms overlapped. And so, we worked through a second literature review, with the objective of combining overlapping terms into a shortlist of overarching headings. Our intent was to better understand their relevance and interrelationship.

Seven key terms emerged as descriptors of 'leadership', as reflected below.

Leadership term	Frequency of appearance
Fulfilment + Values + Risk	150 + 53,071 + 21,078 = 74,299
Strategy	69,899
Communication	54,555
Influence	41,039

Leadership term	Frequency of appearance
Control	34,428
Resilience + Confidence + Determination + Courage	2,458 + 9,212 + 3,735 + 2,431 = 17,836
Empowerment	13,939

With the guidance of Transform Performance International's psychometricians – professionals specializing in the study of educational or psychological measurements – these seven terms formed the foundation of what we identified as the archetypal leader's Destination Beliefs. Further investigations into the seven Destination Beliefs furnished us with an array of accompanying Journey Motivators.

With a framework in place, based on the extensive research and meta-analysis we'd conducted, we were ready to test the hypothesis.

We identified 973 leaders who were willing to engage with the research and form our sample group. These leaders were from 11 different vertical markets and from 17 countries. Some leaders worked with small teams and others were leaders of senior managers and teams of significant numbers. These subjects were selected to provide our study with a representation of leadership performance across four quartiles. Our aim was to map out a 'code' of top-performing leaders that manifests itself in the way they act and can be modelled by anyone who is curious to perform at a higher level. The 973 who participated completed an online questionnaire consisting of 147 questions. Based on a Likert scale used to represent attitudes on a subject, the questionnaire probed their beliefs and attitudes towards the aforementioned seven categories of leadership. This meant that we were able to gather more than 143,000 data points. Our data scientists created an algorithm to filter out any data that was inconsistent and, consequently, had a moderate to high likelihood of lacking integrity. In addition to the core 147 questions, we established filtering criteria that enabled us to analyse differences in any of the following areas or combinations of the following:

1. Gender
2. Geography
3. Vertical market
4. Size of team
5. Leadership tenure
6. Performance

Most of our subjects will have been awarded their leadership role because they have demonstrated proficiency in the leadership 'basket' of skills, behaviours, knowledge and experience that sets them apart from others. This means that the difference between the belief systems of the top performers and lower performers will appear marginal at first glance: and this was exactly what our researchers expected to see. However, a more forensic examination of the data reveals that the top performers display small differences across all measures compared with even the slightly lower performers.

It is the compound effect that we call 'the difference that makes the difference'. This concept has been well publicised in the world of sport and is often called 'the aggregation of marginal gains'. It is human nature to look for, admire and talk about those seminal moments in a competition, when the trophy was won or lost – the moment of great skill from a player, the incident where the referee made a mistake, or even where fate intervened with the weather conditions. However, the aggregation of marginal gains ignores those moments and looks instead to the improvement of decision-making and actions on a day-to-day basis. Those small changes that, over time, add up to a lot. And nearly all those decisions and actions will have taken place long before the final match for the trophy even takes place. The match becomes the culmination of the aggregation of marginal gains over months or even years.

The code that we share in the book is based on the average result of all quartile-one performers. This includes all genders, vertical markets, size of teams, geographies and tenures. To provide a laser-like focus on the results, we have allocated 20 points only to the range where scores were applied by the respondents. This approach is known as 'data sampling' and is a statistical analysis technique used to select, manipulate and analyse a representative subset of data points to identify patterns and trends in the larger data set being examined. It enables data scientists, predictive modellers and other data analysts to work with a small, manageable amount of data about a statistical population to build and run analytical models more quickly, while still producing accurate findings.

The most significant findings were then put to the test.

As we did in *The Salesperson's Secret Code*, alongside our online psychometric questionnaire we identified 13 of the world's most successful leaders. We call them the 'Iconics' because of their significant impact on leadership across a wide spectrum of disciplines, from brain surgery and the National Basketball Association to the English National Ballet and the executive suite at Twitter.

Each Iconic participated in a semi-structured interview, answering a series of very open 'starter' questions in whatever way they liked. Our interviewers used a technique known as *clean questioning*. This involved keeping their own thoughts and assumptions out of the conversation, while matching the subjects' intonation and body language, which put the Iconics at ease and encouraged them to open up. That helped us explore in depth how each leader interprets their own world and how their experiences helped create a structure for their successes. All answers were recorded and transcribed, and the transcripts were analysed using data and language analysis software that flagged commonly repeated key words and ideas.

Every Iconic offered detailed stories about almost daily occurrences where a belief drove a motivation, which prompted a behaviour, that ultimately led to achieving a desired result.

Interestingly, without exception, every Iconic in one way or another referenced the seven Destination Beliefs from our literature review and online questionnaire.

With that understanding of the thinking and process behind the framework, it's time now to briefly explore the Destination Beliefs. Thereafter, a chapter will be dedicated to each of them and we'll explore the relative intensity of the Journey Motivators to reveal the optimal balance in top performers: The Leader's Secret Code.

DESTINATION BELIEFS

You'll know by this point that this book and our study have been about beliefs. The beliefs held by our top-performing leaders drive them to behave in certain ways, and those behaviours lead to specific outcomes.

So, what is a belief?

By definition, a belief is an emotionally held, deep-rooted opinion that we assume to be fact. As we revealed in our previous study, on the attributes of successful salespeople, beliefs provide us with the motivation to deploy certain talents or skills. At the same time, they may promote or inhibit certain behaviours. They have a major impact upon our sense of self, of who we are and why we do what we do. This is why we can observe such marked differences between the low and top performers. It's also why we can readily see why our Iconics have succeeded as they have.

The curious thing about beliefs is that, like behaviour, they can change: what we hold to be true both for ourselves and others are often presuppositions. We presuppose their veracity, act in ways that support the presumption and reinforce the same idea as a belief when we 'discover' that it worked or fulfilled its promise. Such beliefs have been at the root of some of humankind's worst excesses and best moments. When new facts are introduced – for example, when we no longer need to physically visit a shop to purchase a product – these beliefs can be recalculated. When we understand who we really are and where our beliefs come from, we can begin to shape them as we see fit.[12]

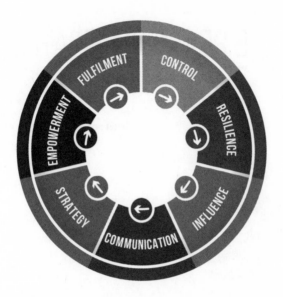

We identified seven Destination Beliefs. For each Destination Belief there are two corresponding Journey Motivators. Each Journey Motivator is 'believed' to a varying degree of intensity.

THE SEVEN DESTINATION BELIEFS UNPACKED

Control is the first component. Top-performing leaders expertly balance the urge to grab the reins with the understanding that, sometimes, others know best. In other words, they don't feel the need to 'know it all'. The requirement of always having to be the smartest person in the room has long dissipated in an era of constant change, mass data and matrixed organizations. Those who understand that leadership doesn't mean having to know everything are generally the most successful at it.

Next, **Resilience** is the ability to bounce back from failure – your own or others' – and it is a key determining factor of leadership performance. Leaders with powerful resilience know when to raise their game to work through difficult times, when

to stop and pivot, when to turn failure into learning and, in equal part, when an entirely unexplored, new approach can best solve a problem.

The next part of our code is **Influence**. After all, what is a leader without followers? Our research has identified two ways leaders view their influential power over others. Some believe that they get things done by encouragement, support and going above and beyond the call of duty. Others hold that their power stems from their position of authority, atop a well-defined organizational structure. In organizations of the future, with their increasingly horizontal structures, it is easy to imagine why high-performing leaders would be more inclined toward the former. The notion of leadership by title alone is doomed as the world moves toward more agile, participative ways of working and traditional organizations flatten and dissolve. It is the collective efforts of the many that will drive success; a real leader understands the power of 'we'.

Going hand-in-hand with Influence, **Communication** comes next. With virtual global workplaces becoming the norm, and multicultural teams often working remotely, the leader who can properly communicate purpose and strategy will conquer. While some leaders

may tend toward clear, unemotional, fact-based messaging, others embrace authenticity, storytelling and glimpses of personal vulnerability at every turn. Top-performing leaders have the ability to combine fact-based messaging with an open, approachable style. The ability to flex style and message depending on the audience and circumstances is a critical attribute for the modern leader.

Next comes **Strategy**, for without strategy a leader is unable to know the way forward. Blending realistic, fact-based plans with their own gut instinct and experience, top-performing leaders shape strategies that will define their business for years to come. They're acutely aware that most strategies will need to adapt to the ever-changing environment, relying on input from those closest to the opportunities and responding to the challenges that inevitably arise. With clear purpose and vision – the adaptively enabling military notion of 'Commander's Intent' – the strategy is delivered by the many, not the few.

And that brings us to the notion of **Empowerment**. A lone leader cannot perform every function and make every decision by themselves. It comes as no surprise, then, that empowerment is an integral part of The Leader's Secret Code. We've found

that the degree to which a leader empowers, delegates and trusts their people to assume accountability and ownership of success (and failure) is directly linked to outcomes.

However, the truly successful leader also limits the extent of others' decision-making and action, deftly balancing leadership, empowerment and shared ownership to build a winning team.

The final part of The Leader's Secret Code is **Fulfilment**. This can be best described as a sense of satisfaction stemming from either believing you have achieved, or are on track to achieve, a personal or professional goal. Research shows that most high-performing leaders are constantly evaluating themselves and their organizations against their goals, and often view organizational and personal success as one and the same. A random conversation with a CEO on a flight back from Zurich provided a revealing and powerful view of fulfilment when he asked, "What will I be known for?" He pondered and answered his own question, saying, "It won't be for increased revenues and EBIT (earnings before interest and taxes), but I hope it's based on the lives I have positively impacted and the legacy that others will continue." Food for thought!

Having identified and defined a range of leadership beliefs, in the next chapter we will see these beliefs in action as we spend time with a group of people from a diverse range of backgrounds, all of whom are successful leaders.

CHAPTER TWO

THE ICONICS

There are quintessentially iconic leaders in every field: those special few held up as unique, different or having a certain *je ne sais quoi* that no one can quite put their finger on. They are the kind of people others are willing to follow into battle and give their all for. We're talking about the kind of leader who naturally takes his or her position at the front, but exists to serve and inspire those around them.

As noted, as part of our research we selected a group of such iconic individuals from a diverse range of backgrounds, with very different experiences and narratives. But they all had one thing in common: they shared the thrill of regular, outstanding success and the devotion of their teams. We were attracted to them not just because they triumph in their particular fields, but because we were led to them via others who held them up as special, inspiring and aspirational. In short, they hold powerful belief systems that distinguish them as winning leaders.

The Iconics we selected embody The Leader's Secret Code. Some are in senior positions; some are excellent managers; and some simply exude leadership qualities in all they do. Some are at the end of their career and some are on their way up. What binds them together is the fact that they have all led, continue to lead and are passionate about leadership and its significance. Their leadership is not limited to boardrooms, sports arenas or battlefields. It's something they embrace in everything they do, including – and one might argue *particularly* – through empowering others to make great things happen.

With that in mind, let's take a close, personal look at our Iconic leaders.

ICONIC 1:
BRUCE DAISLEY
EMEA VICE PRESIDENT, TWITTER

ABOUT BRUCE

Bruce is the EMEA VP for Twitter, and has worked for Google, YouTube and in magazines and radio. He has been one of *The Evening Standard's* 1,000 Most Influential Londoners for four years and is one of *Debrett's* '500 Most Influential People in Britain'. He runs a popular podcast called 'Eat Sleep Work Repeat' and he recently wrote *The Joy of Work: 30 Ways to Fix Your Work Culture and Fall In Love With Your Job Again*, a No. 1 *Sunday Times* business bestseller.[13]

Bruce grew up in what many would say were challenging circumstances and was the first person in his family to go to university. When he graduated, he was rejected time and time again by employers until he drew a cartoon CV of his life that set him on his way.

Bruce is refreshing in that, unlike many social media executives, he is happy to admit that he works for a news company. In fact, he said that its 'breaking news' agenda is why he joined Twitter in the first place.

"Why do you press the Twitter bird on your phone? Principally it's because you want to know what's going on – *the news*," he said. "I'm a news addict. That's the reason why this job is so appealing to me. It's the joy of revelation."

KEEPING IT REAL

Bruce is eccentric for a senior executive and loves a raging debate. For example, the 47-year old rails against the macho culture of bragging about working ludicrously long hours, which is surprising given that he's responsible for all of Twitter's operations across Europe, the Middle East and Africa. He works from the company's London office, which employs 200 people, and advocates working only 40 hours a week. "We've got to this stage where people mistakenly think that the key to success is to get up at 5am, have a breakfast of champions and work out. But how much sleep are these people getting? The need to work longer and harder leads to burnout and exhaustion; I'm interested in the science of that."

He insists that the London set-up is not just a satellite office for Twitter's main operations in Silicon Valley, where company founder and chief executive Jack Dorsey sits. Bruce says Dorsey's a good listener, despite being an introvert, and that they regularly exchange emails and chat. He adds that the UK office has been a leader in changing the business, particularly relative to the management of offensive tweets, partly because of the country's aggressive attitude to pastimes such as soccer.

"The way Twitter is used in different countries strongly varies. Regarding the safety stuff, we (the UK) have always been the ones saying we need to be more vigilant. Look at sport. In the US there is far less emphasis on 'away fans'. In the UK you've always had opposing fans in the stadium and we have more of a history of crowd rowdiness and heckling: so when some elements of that were coming online, we were the first to say we need to be aware of this."

Despite being a Twitter zealot, Bruce is happy to tackle the darker sides of the site, namely the trolling and abuse that takes place. He admits that the company may have been lax on this front in the past but insists it has started to clamp down on the behaviour. "We suspend 10 times more accounts than we did a year ago. We've cleaned up so much, although you'll never fully win on those things. But everyone is focused on making Twitter a good place to have conversations."

Outside Twitter, his big interest is education. He participates in Speakers for Schools, a charity that arranges for successful people to talk to state school children. He believes it is important to have a work network and thinks it's easier for private school pupils to replicate that because they are born into 'the system' via their parents. That's why the charity's key aim is to provide this support to state school children.

Although he says he tries not to work in the evenings, his focus on living a balanced life doesn't seems to include much switched-off downtime. "I've just been writing a book, so I've been finishing edits on that. I have a podcast that I do, and I arrange guests for that, so if I'm chatting to psychologists these are people who have two degrees in psychology and have written multiple books. If I'm interviewing them there's a degree of the amateur interviewing the expert. So, you know, I'll often find myself reading psychology books or things like that, preparing for those podcast interviews."

Bruce's last word on leadership was to recount a recent conversation: "A member of the Special Forces said it's a big fallacy for people to think that there's an abundance of orders – he said the job of a leader in the Special Forces is not to give instructions. It's to agree to a plan and commit to that plan collectively, as a team. He said if you find yourself giving orders all the time, there's been a failure of leadership or there's been a failure somewhere along the line."

ICONIC 2:
CHRIS NEWITT
GLOBAL PERFORMANCE & STEERING DIRECTOR,
JAGUAR LAND ROVER

ABOUT CHRIS

"I genuinely believe that life is unbelievably simple if you want it to be simple. There are a number of things that I try and live by, and one of them is: where there's complexity provide simplicity."

These are the opening words in our interview with Chris, Global Performance & Steering Director for one of the world's most famous brands, the £25 billion automaker Jaguar Land Rover. Chris has accountability for group revenue across all products and services. He knows the automotive sector intimately, having also held senior positions at Skoda and Volkswagen.

"As a leader your job is to get the best out of the people, make the complex simple, where there is confusion provide clarity, and where there is complacency drive energy," he said. "The way I see the world, a team leader's job is to deliver today and to deliver tomorrow, and that, I think, brings the best out of leaders. It brings imagination, different ways of working and different perspectives. Leaders who think tactically will solve a problem today but create a bigger problem tomorrow."

When you operate at Chris's level, life is fast, it requires intellect and it generates an abundance of the VUCA (volatile, uncertain, complex and ambiguous) fog we discussed earlier. He understands from experience that open, transparent communication will simplify life for those on the receiving end, while encouraging them to trust him and make decisions more quickly.

He uses metaphor to simplify his communication and make it more memorable. One example: comparing car manufacturing to chicken sandwiches. Having no sandwiches available on Monday and Tuesday, and then three on Wednesday, is no good for the customer.

"What is the most satisfying is actually less about the end result, and more about having the ability to do whatever needs to be done to the very best of my personal ability," he told us. "It's also about facilitating the team to be able to do the very best job, and that can sound very simple. But it's all too easy to compromise because a bit of the business wants this and a bit of the business wants that, and so on and so forth. And things overlap, and before you know it people are not doing the best job that they can do. They're doing someone else's best job."

Chris is required to engage with the automotive giant's board on a regular basis. He describes his approach to board meetings this way: "In order to guide them through a decision you are telling a story, like it's pitching a film in an elevator. They've got the weight of the world on their shoulders, so you need to be able to take them to the beginning of the journey. But paint the picture of the journey very clearly, very concisely, for a board member because they've got myriad different problems. They've just walked out of a meeting and they're ten minutes late and they're trying to orientate themselves. They know you've presented to them on this before, but it was three months before and they can't remember what it was, so you've got to be able to tell your story in a way that works for them."

He continued: "You've got to be able to give them the confidence that you're not hiding stuff, and that there isn't a hidden rabbit hole that they need to seek and find, and you have got to give them the confidence that the work's been done. But you've also got to try and make their life as easy as possible."

THE HERE AND NOW, AND INTO THE FUTURE

Chris has achieved tremendous success by focusing on delivering results now, while putting in place whatever is required to deliver success in the longer term. Delivering immediate results without regard for longer-term success is relatively easy, but it can paralyse the longer-term position. You often see sporting teams succeeding in the short term and then taking years to recover.

"There aren't really that many difficult problems," he told us. "The difficult problems are the ones that get closer and closer to you, and then climbing the three-foot wall is suddenly quite hard work. If you see it coming a long way off, I've only got to adjust my course by two degrees, and I don't even touch the walls. I think the first step is to see it coming from a long way off."

We've heard a famous leader say that he interrogates the data until it confesses. Chris is also a great believer in the 'truth' being in the data, and that the skill in understanding the true cause of a challenge is what sets the best leaders apart. Along with a forensic-like focus on detail, Chris exhibits high levels of emotional intelligence (EQ) and balance, as he seeks to encourage laughter, empowerment and learning.

"Truth lies in the data rather than people's perceptions," he said. "The perceptions will affect their ability to implement the change, but it doesn't change the root cause of the problem. The correct answer will lie in the data; how you go about it will rest in their perception. The data generally does not lie. You might not like the answer, but it definitely doesn't lie."

Chris believes that you must look at things differently just to stand still, and you have to change just to get the same. In his world this means that looking at what Mercedes and BMW are doing will not set Jaguar Land Rover apart. He would rather seek insight and inspiration from other successful brands and leaders, such as the hotelier Gordon Campbell Gray. As referenced earlier, this might be to understand how a five-star hotel checks its customers in, to learn what Jaguar Land Rover might emulate when booking in car owners for service or repairs.

"No one wants someone at their funeral to stand up and say that they were a great manager and delivered a project in half the time," he said. "You want them to talk about you as a friend, and as a companion, and how you helped change how people felt. Yes, people do remember that we sold 200,000 cars and we did this with you, but what they really remember was how it felt achieving those goals."

Chris focuses himself and his leadership team on doing the best they can each possibly do, rather than focusing on the numbers. This attention to behaviour naturally leads to number delivery as a result, an output, of their activity. If a recalibration is needed, it happens at the behaviour level rather than through a conversation about numbers, which often comes too late.

Chris' last word on leadership focused on humility. "I certainly don't need public recognition, and I'm quite happy with my own company," he said. "I find it quite embarrassing when people are clapping and going, you know, 'Chris, you did a great job'. I might feel differently if I were a doctor saving lives or something, but I'm not."

ICONIC 3:
MAX HILL QC
DIRECTOR OF PUBLIC PROSECUTIONS

ABOUT MAX

We arranged to meet Max Hill QC at the headquarters of the Crown Prosecution Service (CPS), Petty France in the heart of Whitehall, London.

Max is the recently appointed Director of Public Prosecutions (DPP) in charge of 6,000 staff who make up the the CPS, which is responsible for prosecuting criminal cases

that have been investigated by the police and other investi-
gative organizations in England and Wales.

We enter the building early in order to pass through all
security checks including the 'air lock' tube doors. Once
inside we are led to the Director's (Max's) office which is
located adjacent to an open plan section of desks. Max's
office is spacious and airy with views overlooking Bucking-
ham Palace, St James's Park and Wellington Barracks.

We are greeted by Max with a huge smile and firm
hand shake. It is quickly obvious that Max is a man of
immense intellect and curiosity (as a career trial lawyer)
with an insightful radar for understanding what makes
people tick. Max has been involved in some of the highest
profile cases in recent years, which in turn have helped to
refine his ability to find the human story in many of the
challenges he has faced. He recalls (among many) the 21/7
failed suicide bombings trials, the inquest into the deaths
of those who perished during the London 7/7 bombings
and also the multiple murder trials following the tragic
death of 10-year-old Damilola Taylor. He tells us that "the
human element of that story (Damilola Taylor) was always
present where it is not so in some other areas of the law,
and of all the human stories the one that made the most
lasting impression on me was the death of that little boy, I
will never forget that case."

Max has always been clear on his journey and open
-minded as to his destination. "As a student I applied a simple set of principles to the working life I was imagining,"
Max says. "Some of those principles emerged at school",
including a desire to be the best advocate he could be, to
represent those within the profession and to proactively
engage with a variety of charity projects. A close look at

Max's comprehensive resume will outline that all three have been and continue to be achieved. It was Max's appointment as the Independent Reviewer of Terrorism Legislation in 2017 that provided the bridge between life at the self-employed Bar and employed life as the Director of Public Prosecutions.

"What was the appeal of the DPP?" we ask. Max pauses for a second and replies, "It was an irresistible opportunity; it was all about taking a step back from practice in court". When Max became Head of Red Lion Chambers in 2012 he stepped from individual case advocate to leader of 120 people, overseeing their professional workload and personal development. Moving to DPP allowed him to step back further and apply that same curiosity and drive, this time to help 6,000 CPS staff located all over England and Wales. As Max explains, "Being able to step back from the minute detail and look across the whole system is what I found really interesting."

Max's 30-year career as a trial lawyer has certainly taught him how to cope with the sheer scale of any challenge before him. He recounts and lives by the advice he gave to young trial lawyers: "However large the case or massive the size of the task, there is only so much that can happen in a single day and in a single court day. If you have prepared well for the six hours of the next day in court then you know you will get through them. It is tempting to be overwhelmed by the size of the entire proceedings, but it is just a succession of days. Whatever level you are, it is essentially one day at a time and there is only so much that can go right or go wrong in the next 24 hours."

Max understands very clearly that his work will often be scrutinized by government, the press and public alike.

"How do you deal with that constant pressure?" we ask. "It's about being resilient," he replies. "Do the best that *you* can do at every stage of the day, it does not mean the best that anybody else might do, but you have to be focused on maximising your own influence on affairs."

As a new leader Max shared a set of guiding principles that have helped him navigate his first months in office. As we noted them, we also appreciated how transferable they are to any leader trying to navigate their first year's tenure, regardless of sector. Max outlined them as follows:

1. Early identification and connection with the core values and principles that you (as leader) are there to uphold
2. Be positive
3. Be resilient
4. Support and encourage everyone around you
5. Speak well of your organization to anyone who will listen.

A human-centred approach is something that we saw throughout the interviews of the Iconics for this book and Max was no exception. Midway through our interview, Max jumped up from his seat and grabbed a small black A5-sized notebook from the shelf with lots of handwritten notes and protruding coloured Post-it notes.

"I realized that there are critical elements of a business that only an insider knows," Max told us. "I decided on Day 1 of my role as DPP to speak to one member of staff every day."

Max outlined to us that he first spoke to the unions to ensure they were in agreement and helped form the basis as to how he would ask people to engage so that it didn't appear overbearing. Max's little black book contains over 100 interviews with staff in just over six months.

We asked: "How long will you keep this up?"

Without hesitation Max responded: "Someone told me it would take me 25 years to get to everyone but my term in role is five years, so my intention is never to stop."

For some people within the CPS with careers spanning over ten or even 20 years, this is the first time that many have ever spoken directly to the leader of the organization. Max is building staff support and gathering unique insight, the likes of which may never have been achieved since the CPS was created. The power of philosophy over mere gesture is undeniably at work.

Max is authentic, humble and great company, perhaps not a surprise for one of the country's leading advocates. And what would Max's last word on leadership be? Perhaps unsurprisingly he said, "We all start from somewhere and I fondly remember some advice from a very senior judge who once said: "Remember to still be yourself and not to lose sight of yourself, you have been selected to do this job because of who you are and not because of who you might pretend to be."

ICONIC 4:
TAMARA ROJO CBE
ARTISTIC DIRECTOR AND LEAD PRINCIPAL
DANCER OF THE ENGLISH NATIONAL BALLET

ABOUT TAMARA

Tamara was born in Canada, raised in Spain and is now Artistic Director and former Lead Principal Dancer of the English National Ballet. When we met her at the ballet's home, adjacent to the Royal Albert Hall (now located in their new purpose-built facility in London City Island), we were immediately struck by her elegance, poise and quiet, steely confidence.

As soon as we entered her office, she swivelled her chair to face us, sitting bolt upright, and smiled. We suddenly found ourselves adjusting our own body positions and wondered if we were inadvertently mirroring her behaviour. As we'd sat in reception, we observed dancers warming up in corridors, running to classes and pirouetting on the spot.

Tamara is imbued with passion for people, passion for ballet and passion for purpose beyond self. She explained: "The life of a man or woman must have purpose that is bigger than their own self-satisfaction."

Tamara's first experience of ballet might be described as fate, or destiny, or perhaps blind luck. At the age of five, while waiting at school for her mother to pick her up, a teacher invited her into the gym to keep warm. It was there that she encountered something she'd never seen: a ballet class. Not having a TV at home, Tamara often listened to records and danced to entertain herself. She immediately fell in love with the softness of the music and the graceful choreography.

As a deep introvert, she found school to be overwhelming. Ballet was an oasis that allowed her to be herself, not having to interact with others, free to "abstract myself in the research of movement". The irony was that a shy introvert – an only child, a solace-seeking young girl – was to become one of the world's finest principal ballerinas, performing around the world to the adulation of huge, and at times royal, audiences. She turned pro at the age of 16 and by 21 was already the principal ballerina of the English National Ballet, with versions of the *Nutcracker* and *Romeo and Juliet* recreated specifically for her.

PASSION AND PURPOSE

Tamara was definitive on the link between passion, purpose and a strong desire to make a change. As a young girl she was initially horrified to learn that ballet was actually a performance art and not just something one just did quietly, after hours, in the school gym. So how did she reconcile her journey from quiet oasis to the world's largest stages? The answer was in her belief that ballet must be for the masses, regardless of social status, ethnicity or cultural nuance.

"Ballet has no language barriers," she said. "It speaks to the heart as it moves you, as an emotional experience, not an intellectual experience."

And so, it was no surprise for us to learn that it was Tamara who introduced ballet shoes in different colours so they would match dancers' different skin tones. Without fully realizing it, she was using ballet – long seen as an elite art form – as a vehicle for inclusivity. On her decision to join the English National Ballet, she said: "I fell in love with a company that wanted to make life better, not just make beautiful ballet."

Executives rising through the ranks will understand the challenge of having to master their discipline, with competence and expertise, while simultaneously excelling at the ability to lead the overall enterprise, cutting across silos, sectors and geographies. Tamara, too, shares this challenge.

As a principal dancer she focused on the very narrow elements of her performance and training, on mastering her discipline. Before moving to her current role as Artistic Director, she attended a retreat for dance leaders and shadowed another artistic director in order to see all the elements of the company, not just the dance itself.

We asked how she made this often-difficult transition from expert to leader. Once again, she spoke of her strong belief in the bigger picture. "As a dancer I had a passive role," she said. "As a leader of a company I now have the ability to give direction, lead the way, take risk and use my initiative."

For her last word on leadership we posed Tamara this question: do you mind moving from the spotlight to the shadows? As quick as a flash she replied: "I understand where I can have impact, and while that might not look like the most glamorous, juicy or even best paid role I could have, it's the place where I can be most useful."

ICONIC 5:
MICHAEL TOBIN OBE
SERIAL ENTREPRENEUR, AUTHOR AND PHILANTHROPIST

ABOUT MICHAEL

Michael seems to reinvent himself at an astounding rate.

He was CEO of the data centre company Telecity Group plc, is a chairman/non-executive director of at least 15 companies around the world and frequently raises six-figure sums for charity. Talk about focus and dedication! He was awarded an OBE by Queen Elizabeth II for services to the digital economy. He has gone on to write two successful business books: *Forget Strategy, Get Results* and *Live, Love, Work, Prosper.*

"Michael Tobin flies in the face of conventional wisdom," said James Bennet MBE, a director at Ernst & Young. "His leadership approach delivers outstanding business performance and is equally relevant to an entrepreneur, someone taking their first steps into employment or a seasoned manager."

When we met Michael for our interview – at the famous Arts Club in London, at 18.00 on a cold winter's evening – we thought that he'd be slowing down for the day. His first meeting had commenced at 07.00. He eschews a chauffeur-driven car and prefers to travel by bus during the day, rather than the underground, so that he can make calls. After our conversation he was due to have dinner with a well-known journalist and a small group of politicians.

Given his accomplishments, many people would be shocked by Michael's upbringing in one of the toughest and most deprived areas of London: a father in prison, his home firebombed on four occasions and surviving being shot at 13 times. His perspective on this is that he was lucky that only one bullet hit him. His rough and tumble early life helped shape his approach to the challenges he'd go on to face in business, as something to simply deal with and overcome. His first experience turning adversity into opportunity came when, living in a South London squat, he sold old pianos scavenged from abandoned buildings.

We asked Michael what he saw as the key to success. "Believe in the art of the possible," he said. "Success is simply getting up one more time than you go down."

In 2018 he raised a significant amount of money for charity by running 40 marathons in 40 consecutive days. This is a man in his 50s, and not only did he run 26.2 miles a day – day after day, for some six weeks – but he did so at 3.30 in the morning so that he could still put in a full day's work. On many of those mornings he'd give a presentation at the London HQ of his business sponsors before diving into a workday that would stretch into the evening hours.

FACING DOWN A FEAR OF THE UNKNOWN

"I believe that reactive problem solving is fundamental to leadership success," Michael told us. "There was a point where I felt that my leadership team lacked the bravery required to achieve the business vision. I took them swimming with sharks, without being in cages, in the belief that if they could face that fear, how could a business challenge get in their way? Going forward, they could then 'copy and paste' the process they went through with the sharks into business situations."

Michael observed a pattern of leadership behaviour at the end of each quarter when there was a frenzy to close deals, in order to hit and exceed sales quotas. He wanted to change this pattern, so he took key leaders to experience an Olympic bobsleigh run, where if you push harder at the beginning, you'll go faster at the end.

Despite his success, he shows incredible curiosity and has evidently evolved beyond the volatile 21-year-old managing director who believed that the louder you shouted the better leader you were. He believes strongly in the psychology of human behaviour and studying what causes people to do what they do. He takes an almost spiritual approach to certain aspects of leadership and has invested heavily in his own development and that of his associates. He has even invited an Indian Yogi in to work with him and his leadership teams. In this respect Michael is not alone. A number of the Iconics we spoke to emphasized the importance of 'self' and its subsequent link to their ability to lead through others.

Bereft of a role model as a younger man, Michael believes that with a mentor he could have been more successful, more quickly. He now regularly mentors 20–30 people, free of charge, because he's convinced that "we all need it".

At the same time, Michael is quite open about his mistakes and his weakness. "I don't believe in failure and see every bump as a learning," he said. "I'm really proud of myself for admitting all the cock-ups and failures that I've made at home. I've benefited from looking at myself, navel-gazing a bit, and realizing what's in here. My family is super important for me, and my wife is extremely important to me, and I think that's changed my perception of everything. And, you see that I'm quite happy to talk about failure and getting things wrong. Everyone gets it wrong."

We asked Mike for his last word on leadership and he circled back to the importance of family: "You have a series of stakeholders – your company, your employees, your suppliers, but also your family. The real return on investment that a leader can deliver is emotional return. So, when you come home with money, but you don't want to talk or you're angry about something that's happened, you're not returning for shareholders."

ICONIC 6:
JOHN CAMPBELL
MASTER CHEF AND ENTREPRENEUR

ABOUT JOHN

John has earned a reputation as a 'master chef', an entrepreneur and a leader in what most people would acknowledge is one of the most challenging business environments.

Born into a warm, hospitable family in Liverpool, John cooked with his grandmother as a child. She instilled in him a love of quality ingredients and good, simple cooking that remains at the heart of his approach to food. John knew from an early age that he wanted to be a chef, and spent his early career working in some of Europe's finest kitchens. He earned his first Michelin star in 1998, in his first year at Lords of the Manor in Gloucestershire. In 2002, he moved to The Vineyard in Newbury, where he achieved two Michelin stars by 2007.

He opened The Woodspeen, his own restaurant and cookery school, in 2013. John's recipes and articles have appeared in magazines and newspapers, including *The Sunday Times*, *Delicious*, *The Observer Food Monthly*, *Food Arts*, *Caterer* and *Hotelkeeper*. He regularly appears at food festivals and on television shows in the UK and abroad, including as a guest judge on BBC's *MasterChef*. Among his many achievements, John authored the cookbook, *Formulas for Flavour: How to cook restaurant dishes at home*.

John has developed a broad and balanced ability to process data to the highest standard across the range of senses. He sees things that others don't and has an uncanny ability to hear, feel, smell and, particularly, taste things. This helps him to coach and mentor, as well as to create distinctive experiences for his customers. He has built a set of beliefs and a workplace culture that align with the following observation, made by, among others, the poet Maya Angelou and Carl W. Buehner: people will forget what you say, people will forget what you do, but people will never forget how you make them feel.

We asked John what a high-performing leader looks like to him.

"I believe that leaders achieve better outcomes more quickly by asking clever questions so that those they lead make better decisions," he said. "Setting rigid rules means that teams will limit their achievements to what they are told to do, so I am a strong believer in giving others the freedom to fail. There's no such thing as failure; it is all learning."

Most people would see the creation of Michelin-starred experiences as extraordinarily complex and nerve-racking. Yet, the celebrity chef seems unfazed by it all. "The simplicity of my approach is basic, and it's human, and that's all it is," he says. Through it all, John exudes a calmness, consistency and trustworthiness that leads others to adopt a similar mindset – a belief in the art of the possible.

AUDIENCE SEGMENTATION

John recognizes that each unique audience requires, and will respond to, a different approach. As such, he seeks to communicate and engage with various groups in ways that will have the most positive effect. For example, with his senior management team he will be more challenging, and set the bar higher, with a focus on the aggregation of incremental gains. He recalibrates these behaviours for more junior teams, with whom he's all about taking time, listening and offering positive encouragement. With certain external audiences he seeks to inspire, sharing insight from the heart. And with his customers, the focus is on understanding how his team can deliver a '10 on a scale of 10' experience, every time.

John talks a lot about giving, and he has a strong desire to help team members achieve their dreams. His business has made significant investments in the local community, working for example with young women from abusive relationships, building their confidence and teaching them how to cook for their children. John is also part of a collaborative effort with the UK's National Health Service (NHS) to help patients get better more quickly. The concept is simple. If you have good food in hospital then it's more likely that you will recover faster, be discharged sooner than might otherwise be the case, and save the NHS money and resources. It also means that beds are freed up to treat more patients. He shows slight frustration at the disjointed nature of overall patient care. "The clinicians know what they are doing. The chefs know what they are doing. But nobody sews it together. This costs the NHS money. We are working on a technological solution that helps keep food moist and palatable for 30, 40, 50 or even 60 minutes." It is clear that John likes to be a well-organized leader. It seems that John likes spending money, but not on himself; and the only time he really spoke about himself was to say that he was interested in learning to play the piano.

John and his team embrace a strong set of principles and beliefs that inspire them and have an incredible impact on all stakeholders. For instance, when we asked him for his final thoughts on leadership, he returned to his vision for the cookery school: "We need to be – and we will be – the best in this country – full stop. We will be the best school in this country and then Europe. We will be the only choice to teach you." An emphatic last word.

Who wouldn't want to be a part of that?

ICONIC 7:
JOHN AMAECHI OBE
PSYCHOLOGIST AND FORMER NATIONAL
BASKETBALL ASSOCIATION PROFESSIONAL

ABOUT JOHN

John is a psychologist, *New York Times* bestselling author and 'Everyday Jedi'. Having grown up in England and the US, he played American high school and college basketball and went on to play professionally in the National Basketball Association (NBA).

However, when we met John, who by his own admission is "six-foot-nine on a good day," he quickly reminded us that "I was just an overweight kid from Stockport who liked pies and books." Yet, as the eldest of three children, he credits his mother with instilling in him a strong belief system.

"I remember her saying the most unlikely of people in the most improbable of circumstances can become extraordinary," he recalled.

John has many vivid memories of his colourful career to date, many of them built on international experiences. Born in Boston and raised in Stockport, Manchester, he played professional basketball in the US, France, Italy, Greece and the UK. With international opportunity came exposure and increased awareness of different people and cultures. Much of John's insight has been built on these experiences as he listened, watched and interacted, just as his mother had carefully listened, watched and – when necessary – nudged him in the right direction.

We could have spoken with John for hours, as his humour and humility led us from story to story. And to be honest, we couldn't help but be a little in awe of the fantastic photograph of him with President Obama that stood proudly framed next to his sofa. One such memory John shared was of training in the gym with his NBA team at the time. He remembers that, as he could feel himself starting to take things easier, one of his coaches whom he admired greatly, discreetly tapped him on the shoulder and whispered, "You're always being observed."

THE ROLE OF THE ROLE MODEL

Today, as John works with leaders across sectors and geographies, he often recalls the coach's remark. "A good leader recognizes that he or she is constantly under scrutiny," he said, "and everything they do matters."

When we explained the focus of The Leader's Secret Code, John shared a belief system that left no doubt about his approach to leadership. He explained his thinking around winning new business: "I'm not interested in winning by one, as winning by one creates a challenge down the road where next time, we face you, you think there's a possibility that you can win, which impacts your chances of winning positively," he said. "That's a problem for me, the thought that I need to beat you in such a way that you are so demoralized by the defeat that when you see me on your schedule – when you see me competing against your organization for a request for proposal or anything else – you don't even bother, because I need you to understand you are beaten before we start."

We asked John about his thoughts on the individual leader. "Leadership is all about personal exertion," he said, "not infrastructure." He went on to suggest that for most organizations, "personal comfort of senior or influential people, or at least the avoidance of personal discomfort of those individuals, trumps organizational performance every single time."

In other words, leadership actions will determine organizational performance, every time.

Another part of John's successful belief system is his constant focus on people: who they are, how they feel and how he proactively interacts with them, to help them become and achieve almost anything. "If a fat kid from Stockport can play in the NBA, then surely anything is possible," he said with a laugh.

We talked about Journey Motivators and Destination Beliefs, and John was deeply reflective, as any leader should be. "I know when I shout, I lose my people for a week," he said. We ask when he last shouted, and he didn't miss a beat: "Thirty years ago."

A common theme in this book and which arose throughout our interviews with the Iconics, is the necessity – and the power – of learning. What have we done? What have we learned? What are the parallels and overlaps? Indeed, many of our iconic leaders base their beliefs and actions on the bedrock of the lessons they've learned.

As John told us: "For any negative experience that you've had there is a positive way to learn a lesson. But remember, you don't have to be beaten up at school to learn resilience."

And John's last word on the subject of leadership? "Learning takes effort and leadership is *energy expensive*," as John put it. "Yet," he said, "it's entirely worth it if you want to emanate an environment around you that allows people to deliver optimally."

ICONIC 8:
MAJOR JAMES KNIGHT MC
ROYAL MARINES

ABOUT JAMES

James has a Military Cross, which is awarded by the British Armed Forces for acts of exemplary gallantry during active operations against the enemy. The best way to properly introduce James is to share what Brigadier John Ridge, the UK's Chief of Joint Force Operations, said of him:

"James worked as my Military Assistant for 18 months. I was responsible for commanding the UK's Extremely High Readiness crisis response headquarters and James' role was to run my outer office and, when deployed, to coordinate my tactical command HQ. He was a superb assistant. Not only did he run the office extremely efficiently, he also took on a huge number of additional jobs, most at his own initiative. He actively sought out people to form an informal crisis network across government and the civilian sector and was perfectly suited to this task because he has exemplary emotional intelligence and easily forms professional relationships with others."

"James also attended the vast majority of my meetings, whether with senior military officers, ambassadors or foreign military staff. He wrote these meetings up and then ensured that key decisions were passed onto the relevant personnel in my HQ. All of this happened without any prompting from me and he regularly had to read between the lines of the meetings to identify the important issues. He never once put a foot wrong."

"James was a first-class (Military Assistant) when the headquarters deployed on Operation Ruman, the UK's disaster response to Hurricanes Irma and Maria in 2017. He headed up my tactical HQ team of five, always ensuring that I understood what was going on in the deployment, that I always had communications with my main HQ and my subordinate commanders, and that our hectic schedule flying around the area of operations was properly coordinated. James is a supremely professional individual, who sets extremely high standards for himself and others. He is proactive and impeccably reliable. Above all, he is a thoroughly decent human being, with a rock-solid moral compass. He knows what is right and will do it, irrespective how difficult that might be."

To round things out, Ridge called James "one of the most popular officers in the HQ, with an excellent sense of humour and a willingness to lend a hand to help others out".

When he was awarded the prestigious Military Cross, it was like pulling teeth to get him to discuss the news with us. When he did, he downplayed his role and focused entirely on attributing the accolade to his men. When the award was given, he wrote individually to each member of the tour to congratulate them. He clearly gets a much greater sense of fulfilment from seeing others succeed than from his own success.

"It's not quite as romantic because it's kind of your job, and there is a British sense that we're just getting on with it," James said. "You're just going through your routine of getting ready and you're not really thinking about what could happen. I must admit, all my experiences were just basically this kind of real British sense of duty, of plodding through it in a sort of dark humour way."

Asked if he didn't derive some personal satisfaction from the honour, he thought for a moment. "I suspect maybe there is 10% of me that would want some recognition along the way," he said. "But when you see the people around you get rewarded for what they've done, that's a really nice feeling. We were very lucky, but I had probably the best troop sergeant in the entire unit working for me. Then I probably had one of the other two best sergeants at the time – another fantastic sergeant. I had a great bunch of blokes. It was on behalf of everyone on that tour."

IT'S EVERYBODY'S COMPANY

As we spoke, he continued to turn the conversation toward others.

"Regardless of my rank and regardless of the youngest marine's rank, it was everyone's company. It was our company and I really wanted that to be the feel, in the tone of the culture. You can have some people that love to operate with complete autonomy. 'Just tell them what the end state is and let me get on with it.' And then you've got other people at the other end of the spectrum. 'This is what the end state looks like, but I'm going to drip-feed you markers along the way and you're going to work toward them.'"

James liked to bring in everyone in his command group and sit them down together, eight or nine people, including the sergeant major, troop commanders, troop sergeants and company quartermaster. The idea was for them to feel that they had a say, and that the team ultimately arrived at a joint decision on how to address a problem.

James has simplified his existence to five white shirts, two pairs of blue trousers and one pair of shoes. He believes that this allows him more energy and brain capacity to focus on more important matters. For instance, he frequently leads groups of young men who might die on any given day. James dismissed the idea that that was a formidable challenge: "This is what we're trained for."

He said that they focus on the objectives, and again suggested that this was perhaps simply a British cultural attribute – 'just get on with it'.

He found climbing a 30-foot rope challenging, and to build physical strength he did 1,000 press-ups a day. His other coping strategy was to confuse the mind by not looking at the top and aiming to climb halfway.

"Climbing a 30-foot rope, that was my nemesis," he said. "It only takes about 30 seconds, but there's a 30-mile run we have to do in seven hours that I'd rather do any day of the week instead of climbing this bloody rope. I used to look at the top, and as I was climbing it felt like I'd been climbing it for hours. And I look up and I was only half-way up. Then the instructor said, 'Right, just go halfway.' And I didn't look up, and before I knew I'd hit the top."

As people with no personal experience leading troops in combat, we'd imagined (after so many hardboiled war movies) that it was centred on barking orders. In reality, James' leadership style couldn't be farther from that, as he focuses on listening and engagement. His sense of curiosity is wide and deep, and it's most pronounced when he's seeking to understand his men – who are they, what motivates them and why they do what they do.

He believes in engaging with his team because they will have valuable ideas and talents, and he is quite open about not having all the answers. He sums this up nicely in a sentence: "Be interested, not interesting."

Of this continuous deep-dive immersion with his team, he said: "They'll throw your train off the tracks, consume a large amount of your time, and consume you emotionally as well. Quite draining, some of it ... because it's all quite good."

At the end of our discussion, rather than ask him for his final thoughts on leadership, we inquired once more about James' award of the Military Cross. "What was it for, specifically?" we asked. He showed little reaction, other than a slight smile, which we would have missed had we blinked at that moment. "Some things are best left unsaid," he replied. This was his last word. That, it seemed, was all the insight we were going to be given on that score. Afterwards we reflected that James displayed, with understated elegance, the very qualities which make him a leader: he is, to his very core, trustworthy and brimming over with integrity.

ICONIC 9:
PETER LEES
CHIEF EXECUTIVE AND MEDICAL DIRECTOR
AT THE FACULTY OF MEDICAL LEADERSHIP
AND MANAGEMENT

ABOUT PETER

Peter is Chief Executive and Medical Director at the Faculty of Medical Leadership and Management (FMLM), an intercollegiate professional body that promotes excellence in leadership on behalf of all doctors in the United Kingdom.

The faculty was established in 2011 by all the medical royal colleges and faculties, with endorsement from the Academy of Medical Royal Colleges (AoMRC). As a professional body charged with setting and maintaining standards, it plays an important role in positioning medical leaders as skilled professionals. The faculty's founding principle was that medical leadership would have to become a true professional discipline if it hoped to effectively deal with challenges facing the UK's health service.

Over 20 years, Peter combined a career in neurosurgery with senior roles in operational management and leadership development. This included experience working at local, regional and national levels and in the global healthcare sector. He previously was Medical Director, Director of Workforce and Education and Director of Leadership at NHS South Central Strategic Health Authority, as well as Senior Lecturer in Neurosurgery at the University of Southampton. In 2017, Peter was appointed Honorary Visiting Professor at Cass Business School, City University, London. He is a graduate of Manchester and Southampton universities, a Fellow of the Royal College of Surgeons of England, a Fellow of the Royal College of Physicians, London, as well as a Founding Senior Fellow of FMLM.

When we sat down with Peter in his very regal London office, we asked, "What do you think makes a high-performing leader?"

"Those working in the medical profession rarely want to be known as leaders," he told us. "Few doctors are interested in the top jobs!" In a 2018 survey of medical directors by Monitor, the public body responsible for making the UK health sector 'work for patients', just 10 of 106 respondents saw chief executive as a possible career move.

We asked Peter to explain why, and he said a big disincentive was the UK's predilection for naming supposedly guilty people when things go wrong. One example he cited was the Stafford Hospital scandal, which came to public attention following an investigation by the Healthcare Commission in 2008. The case revealed appalling conditions, substandard care and a high patient mortality rate. As a result, Martin Yeates, chief executive of the Trust that was responsible for running the hospital, was suspended, while its chair, Toni Brisby, resigned. Both Prime Minister Gordon Brown and Health Secretary Alan Johnson apologized to those who had suffered – or worse – at the hospital.

"This whole scapegoating – taking one person, giving them an impossible job, and then publicly humiliating and sacking them – you don't need to be clever to work out that this is not a great recruiting approach," Peter said. "Do we really want to have a system where we're pretty well alone in the Western world with virtually no doctors going into chief executive roles, when it's often the norm in Europe and the States? With many trusts now in breach of waiting time and financial targets, the job of chief executive is increasingly likely to end in failure. Not only are the problems big and growing, but trust managers have limited power to tackle underlying causes, such as chronic shortages of general practitioners."

We asked Peter if his interest in leadership started at medical school, or was something that he developed over time.

"I suppose when I look back over my early clinical career, I had always tried to make things more efficient. In fact, I was driven mad by inefficiency, so I got involved in many initiatives over those years to address these problems.

But back then we would never have known that you called it management or leadership. I think there is something inherent in a medical leader having reached a certain level of experience in the system that then actually makes you better equipped in making decisions – otherwise you've simply become a manager who happens to have a medical degree. If, as has been suggested, we need to get more doctors into chief executive positions, we may have to rethink things. I still think there's a lot to be gained from having a significant clinical career."

THE EXPERTS' EDGE

Research by the Cass Business School backs that up, he said. "In a variety of settings they have shown that 'experts' have the edge on non-experts. For example, they showed that card-holding academics make more successful vice chancellors. They also showed that there is a 25% quality premium associated with medical chief executives."

We then spoke with Peter about whether he thought there was an optimal, or minimal, level of training needed to be a successful leader.

"I don't think anybody knows the answer to that, but we are making progress. First, we have to recognize that at all levels of a clinical career, leadership requirements, roles and responsibilities change. It then becomes evident, unless you're deluded into thinking that leaders are born, that individual doctors at every level need help to develop and hone their skills commensurate with the level they are operating at."

Our discussion then moved to a recent piece in the medical periodical *The BMJ*, in which Peter advocated for a flatter hierarchy in the profession. We asked how junior doctors and medical students interested in leadership and management can pursue that ambition.

"I think it depends on which roles you mean," Peter said. "If you think you can ask a medical student to take on the medical director role, the answer is you can't. But what I think we should be doing, which is starting to happen, is giving medical students and junior doctors appropriate training and development to help them develop these skills. The second thing I'd say is that you don't need some sort of formal title of *leader* to actually be doing it. So, medical students to a lesser extent, but all junior doctors are leaders in their own right. Finally, as part of seeking ways to develop people in the medical profession, we need to be much more creative in giving students and trainees opportunities to lead."

He said the profession needs to be much more aware of the leadership already undertaken by junior colleagues who lead when they interact with patients, and who have to lead if they are the most senior member of a team. "For example, on a daily basis the first person at a cardiac arrest leads," he said. "I think it's important to help everyone in the profession understand the importance of a combination of clinical experience and leadership. If they get the leadership bit wrong, the patients will suffer, and if they get the clinical bit wrong, the patients will suffer. The answer is to create opportunities to develop people earlier in their careers, which we do to some extent through the fellowships scheme, which melds leadership responsibility and experience."

What was Peter's final thought on leadership? After a pause he replied somewhat wistfully, "We've got to get away from this rather outdated notion that you've got to be old and grey before you do anything around developing leadership. We're wasting masses of talent by that approach."

ICONIC 10:
VARDA SHINE
FORMER CEO OF DE BEERS
DIAMOND TRADING COMPANY

ABOUT VARDA

We first met Varda during a series of leadership pro-grammes for global tech leaders in Silicon Valley. Varda was the highlight of the programme as her sense of humil-ity, purpose and resilience was always clear for the young leaders to see, hear and embrace.

Our meeting with Varda for this book took place on an unusually cold and wet London morning in June. Varda was in between international assignments coaching execu-tives from around the world.

Varda grew up in Israel, completed her military service and quickly found herself working in the diamond busi-ness. Who could have known then that she would go on to become a CEO?

Varda made her view of the importance of people immediately clear to us. "No matter how good you are you will never achieve things without people," she said.

We asked: "What makes a good leader?"

Varda paused for a second and answered: "Values. Integrity is my number one value."

She also listed self-awareness, humility, the need for constant communication and honesty with people as criti-cal ingredients of the modern leader.

"You can't do anything if you don't have people with you. Being authentic and being you, without playing games, was very important to me and this led me over the years."

One of Varda's greatest challenges as CEO was mov-ing the company's operations from London to Botswana. "When we agreed the move to Botswana, I actually communicated this to staff two years in advance. It was clear that not everyone was going to relocate, but I still needed people to continue working for those two years.

Being very honest is really important; if people don't know what is going on, they start to make assumptions and a lot of times those assumptions (in their head) are much worse than the reality."

Varda has always acted with the same focus toward the organization too. "Being Israeli I call things as they are, I am not a corporate politician and don't play games. I may have been refreshing at a time when the company was doing well. When a company is doing well it can become quite numb. I was calling out things I saw or things I thought need calling attention to. I was different, for sure."

This approach coupled with a direct style of communication ensured that the Diamond Trading Company (DTC) was more than just about finances. "People want to work for an organization that has a vision beyond making money for shareholders. There must be a higher purpose and something they can relate to, especially in an ambiguous workplace."

Varda made it clear that the organizational purpose was important for the people working within it, especially as "the best employees are people who have other options but choose to stay working with you".

"What was a seminal moment for you at De Beers?" we asked.

"How we reacted to the 2008 crisis," Varda replied. "We were 1 billion short of our target in quarter four of 2008. In quarter one of 2009, we were all thinking about solutions but there was a real buzz. We asked our clients and staff to work together and collaborate to create the solution. We gave the clients the confidence that we were still investing in marketing, and I remember our messaging was clear. 'There are two things that last longer than life:

love is one of them. A diamond is forever.' By May 2009 the diamond industry was out of the crisis and the price of diamonds went up and up."

When we asked, "What themes come up most often with the senior executives you have been coaching?" Varda paused momentarily, before replying: "A lot of the conversations are about people. I remember the first time I had to let someone go changed me as a leader. It was a small office and I knew the guy needed a job. But as much as it pained me to do that, it was the best thing that could have happened to him. He ended up 'reinventing' himself and I learned to trust myself and my relationship with people to make sure that I do it the right way. You have to give people real, honest feedback. So I'm very open with people. I believe in telling people what you see, where things stand, explain your point of view and then look at the possibilities."

We asked Varda for her last thoughts on leadership. "With people issues being an essential focus for any CEO, it's possible that too many of them also fall into the trap of meeting overload," she said. "They run from one meeting to another without the time to stop, to reflect and actually think quietly, or to seek people's opinions and listen."

ICONIC 11:
ALEXANDRA ALTINGER
CEO UK, EUROPE AND ASIA AT
JO HAMBRO CAPITAL MANAGEMENT

ABOUT ALEXANDRA

We met with Alexandra in the offices of Duke CE London having previously worked with her on a series of leadership events during previous months. Alexandra had just completed four years as the CEO of Sandaire Investment Office.

Since the interview she has become CEO UK, Europe and Asia at JO Hambro Capital Management.

When we met Alexandra, we were struck by her quiet, assured confidence. Always impeccably dressed, Alexandra speaks softly yet with focus. She is Italian and German, and was born in the US, yet grew up in Europe. As a kid she remembers moving countries almost every three years due to her father's job, learning to speak four to five languages by her early teens and making new friends so frequently it became second nature. She realized as a teenager that while she wanted to fit in and be like everyone else, she simply wasn't. "It took time for me to come to terms with the reality that I was different and when you own that, it's quite liberating," she said.

After university at the age of 22, Alexandra decided to purchase a one-way ticket to Japan to follow her passion for Japanese culture coupled with the allure of a career in finance. This was in 1991, a time where there was limited access to mobile phones and the internet. She stayed in Tokyo where she worked as a trader for two and a half years.

"It was a hard and lonely experience being one of very few foreign women in Japan at the time," she said. But her early years had already proved to her that she "had the need to do something different in order to succeed".

What was obvious to us during this interview, was Alexandra's unwavering spirit of individualism, perhaps an essential ingredient for resilience?

To this she responded: "If I take the hard and unconventional choice and succeed, I know it will make me stronger and that will make me more resilient just like a muscle you develop. It's only by taking the choices that are not the obvious ones, and then accepting you will struggle, fall down, trip up, be humiliated, sometimes even feel like a complete failure ... but then you just get yourself back up again and get on with it, that's how you build resilience, because no one can teach you resilience: it's not theoretical."

Resilience proved an essential strength for Alexandra during her first years as CEO, much more so than a high IQ or EQ score.

"You need to go into that office every single morning and believe what you are doing is right and no matter what gets thrown at you, you will navigate the business through it. You have to be that constant in a whole sea of movement and uncertainty. People look up to you, people seek your guidance, people look at the expression on your face every day ... and however you are feeling you have to go in and be strong and absolutely confident in what you are doing. As the leader, people look to you for reassurance that the ship is being properly steered in the right direction ... I learn from every challenge, it's something I constantly seek out, it makes me feel alive, it makes me grow."

As a successful CEO and mother of five, Alexandra knows that her wisdom has come from many places. "I'm uncompromising in terms of outcome and tend to be very clear on my vision and values but you have to let people do things in their own way. I learned this from my children. As a parent you can't control all that your children do but you can be clear on your expectations for them."

Alexandra epitomizes the ethos of strong values, loosely held. "A good leader needs to be clear on the vision and the outcomes and define the milestones along the way and then give people the latitude and freedom to achieve those milestones in their own way."

She is also very clear on the need for constant strategic focus. "Anyone can set strategic objectives, but very few understand good strategy. So many people make the mistake of confusing objective setting (targets) with strategy. Defining the target is easy, but the journey is difficult. It's not the strongest, biggest or fastest one that wins, it's the most strategic that wins. Strategic thinking will help you gain superiority."

Alexandra is a strong, passionate and proactive advocate for female leadership. "As a woman, people make assumptions about you or expect you to lead like a man. It's not about projecting force, strength or imposing your approach, sometimes it's about being subtle and building relationships and getting implicit buy-in. This takes longer but can be far more effective."

Her drive is palpable but so is her authenticity, humility and inclusive nature. This is borne out by her answer when we asked her for her last word on leadership. "To help people feel validated you need to empower them and ensure they feel empowered, or you will never get the best out of them. Being empowered is not same as *feeling* empowered. You can give someone a title but if that person doesn't feel empowered then they simply won't act empowered. Part of feeling empowered that is they must feel comfortable to try something new, to make mistakes, comfortable to speak up and to have a different opinion, to feel validated and know that their views count. It's about creating a whole inclusive culture around individuals so that they truly feel valued."

ICONIC 12:
KAREN PENNEY
VICE PRESIDENT, PAYMENTS PRODUCTS
UK WESTERN UNION BANK

ABOUT KAREN

When we sat down with Karen her ability to put people at ease was apparent from the start. She exuded an aura of calmness, a certainty about what she was about to do. We asked her about this. "I am pleased you noticed," she replied. "I think it is important to prepare. You show respect for your subject. You show respect for those who are meeting with you. It also means that you create more energy. For example, I held a meeting last week for the sales team. They all said that the day went so fast and was so energetic. I am sure that the reason for the team's reaction was down to the preparation. It is something I have worked on as I have gone through my career. When meetings are more engaging, I can give everyone a voice. Everyone knows what is expected before the meeting and that means when we are in the meeting we are all fully present and knowing what we need to achieve."

We were interested to understand some of the driving forces behind Karen's leadership behaviours. What were her earliest leadership influences? "My father is a role model. He was a professional footballer in the days before they earned the big money. When he stopped playing, he managed teams and I always noticed that, whether his teams won or lost, he always reacted in the same way. Of course, he celebrated the wins, but he was never put off by the losses. To this day I cannot contemplate an environment where the leader is not calm and displays inconsistency. My father was also an accountant and he got me some work experience at an investment house. On my first day I came out of Bank station in the City of London and thought, 'Yes! This is where I want to be.' There were smartly dressed people scurrying around going off to do very important things in glittering towers. I think I was also influenced by the TV show, *Capital City*, where they were all massively glamorous. But it was also because there were problems to solve and they sat together and worked things out to a successful conclusion. They made a difference."

Making a difference is important to Karen. "I believe in making an impact and I like things to happen quickly. In large organsations things tend to be done consecutively. We wait for one thing to finish before moving the next stage. I want to change things, to challenge the way things are. For example, rather than do things in sequence, why not look at how we can do things in parallel? That, for me, has been a real driver and I try to encourage my people to think that way. For example you might not have signed up a client yet, but there is no reason why you cannot do certain background checks in preparation for onboarding them. In my current role we have already shortened the sales cycle dramatically by adopting a new perspective on speed of thought and action. I have noticed that when I ask my team a question they are already saying, 'Yes we have thought of that and are already on it.' When this happens it's fantastic because you know you are having a positive impact on your people and on your business."

Karen began her career in the banking industry and has held numerous senior roles, most recently at American Express and, at the time of writing, Western Union Bank. The financial services sector was traditionally dominated by men in leadership positions and, although this is now changing, we wondered what impact this has had on Karen's leadership style. "Well, I don't think it's a gender thing at all. I have worked for male leaders who are very approachable and female ones who are far from it.

I try to model the good in all I see. One male leader I worked for, for 15 years, asked me once if I remembered the day we met. He was able to describe in detail that first encounter and my first impression upon him. Since then I have tried to recall as much as I can about people I meet – their families, the names of their kids and so on. I have always been so impressed by people who just seem to be able to pick up where we left off."

We asked if Karen feels that she is a carrying the torch for women in senior positions. She paused for a moment. "I'd like to think that I am a role model for other women. It is not something I have sought. I try to have balanced teams and I try to encourage women as much as I can – women are tough on themselves. We don't put ourselves forward enough or sing our own praises. We don't look at the job description and say, 'Yes I can do most of that.' We worry about the one area that we have not covered and often walk away. A lot of women look for perfection, but perfection is not needed. Very good is good enough! Most of us are not joining up nerves in people's brains. If a bullet point is not totally aligned it's not a big deal. The content of a presentation is far more important. I am not an evangelist for women, but I try it help where I can; and if I can share any thoughts or ideas then I am happy to do so. I think men are better at dealing with imposter syndrome than we are. We females are cautious about putting ourselves forward. Having said that, we can be just as judgemental as the next person. I even heard my own mother the other day saying that someone needed to 'man up'! It is inculcated into us. I was lucky – my parents encouraged me to give everything a go, but even I get those 'inner voices'. I can be on a stage as the inspirational speaker of the day and I hear the voices

– 'Why should she be here talking to us? Who does she think she is?' Those nerves are always there. On the other hand, they keep you on your toes. You prepare well. Ah! Back to preparation again."

BE APPROACHABLE; BE AUTHENTIC; BE NICE

We asked what words of advice to aspiring leaders Karen would offer. Without hesitation she said, "Two A's: approachability and authenticity. And an N, for nice. Let me share why being approachable is so important to me. I had a situation when someone was seriously mentally ill. I did not know them and they'd been off work for some time. The situation ended really sadly and, in all my time leading people, they were one of the few people I did not know. I'm not saying that I could have changed the outcome, sad though it was, but I could have had more input into the situation; perhaps given different perspectives which might, just might, have changed things. Since that time I have tried to be even more approachable than I was previously. I spend most of my time with my team. In a fast moving place like Western Union I am with the team and available to the team as much as I can be – email, mobile and so on – I try to be there. And I want to be available to them for both professional and personal issues. It's essential that I am approachable and that no one fears any kind of retribution for simply being open with me. If you asked most people who have worked for me I am confident they'd say I am approachable. I am in no doubt as to the positive impact this trait has had on the results I have driven in my various commercial roles."

"Being authentic is absolutely essential in leadership. I think it's important to show an interest in every individual, to be naturally curious. I have been told often that this is one of my key strengths. To me, that curiosity is authenticity. Most people can sniff it out when you are not being real. This will happen throughout your career. Someone came to me the other day for guidance. She had recently had her first baby and was struggling with other calls on her time in relation to her work. I said, 'I know exactly what you mean. Why don't you consider just putting work on hold for a while? You don't need to do everything all at once.' She looked at me and said, 'I feel so much better. I thought I was doing something wrong, but you are showing me I am just normal.' She just wanted someone to relate to her situation and to give her the power and the permission to do what she needed to do. The sharing of what's happened to you is so important. When things are not going well people need to see how you cope and even show your vulnerability. It's vital to show that you are human. I had a friend who managed a call centre and it had to downsize. She cried the day she had to lay people off and, although I don't advocate women crying daily at work, in that moment and in those circumstances it was actually the right thing to do. It's about showing the right emotional intelligence and managing one's feelings and relationships in the right way. I graduated from Oxford with a degree in English and went to work for a large UK bank. In those days when the branch manager walked past you pinned yourself up against the wall to allow him (and it was a him) through! You genuflected in his presence. I knew his name and nothing more about him. He knew nothing of me. Any leadership I got then was from people below him in the rankings. No, having an aloof leader and someone who cannot, or will not, engage is not helpful, especially in today's world.

Also way back in my career I was more reluctant to share personal stories. These days I share a lot and I think it is fair to share these things with others so that they can consider alternative perspectives. And feedback is sharing and that is very important. I seek it and I give it. If others decide to reject it that is fine. I simply offer my perspective from a position of complete authenticity."

"And as for being nice to others, it's just a good way to be. You know, when I first started my career I was so determined to get on and do well I did not consider the people around me. And I had to learn that. As I have gone through my career I have met people in different places and I have had people follow me. Don't focus on yourself, just do the right thing by others and the right things happen. I have a general sense of right and wrong, about acting with integrity and how one should behave towards others. I think I have an inbuilt desire to enjoy my life and make it as pleasant as possible for others along the way. It does not mean being weak or a pushover, but there is enough bad stuff going on in the world and there is no reason for me to add to it!"

A BREATH OF FRESH AIR

Our final question to Karen was this: imagine yourself at the end of your leadership career. What would you want to hear other people say about you? Karen leaned back in her chair and a closed her eyes momentarily. Then she moved forward, purposefully. "First," she said, "I would want to hear people say that I had been challenging and passionate. I think passion is important. I see it in the new young people I am bringing into the business. It is infectious. They encourage the more tenured people to think differently.

When people are challenged in the right way it's great. Give people the freedom to try out new ideas, look to the future, futureproof your business. Ask them, what are the trends? What is coming down the line? What will make you stand out to your customers? All of these things present challenge and they can be addressed and resolved with passionate people around you."

"Next I'd like to hear people say that I was creative and that I left a mark that the organization did not have previously wherever I worked. I have found that moving organization has given me freedom to think about things differently. I have always enjoyed the roles I have had. I have been lucky and played to my strengths, rather than worry about my weaknesses. I have learned how to develop, but have always focused on my strengths. Most of us don't do jobs which are life and death situations. We can be creative and have some fun doing it. If something goes wrong it's a learning opportunity and not a total and utter disaster."

"Finally, I would be proud to hear others say that I was a breath of fresh air in an organization. It does not matter what level you are in a business. Always ask yourself how you differentiate yourself from the person who did your role previously. I had a role in a previous life which had been all about spreadsheets. When I took it on I knew I did not have those skills so I set about bringing a new perspective which was about why we had all that data in the spreadsheet in the first place. What was it doing for us, for customers? How was it interesting? In short, I changed the way the role was considered. You bring a freshness. Anyone can do that. You become the role model for others."

ICONIC 13:
SARAH EBANJA
CEO TOTTENHAM HOTSPUR
(SPURS FC) FOUNDATION

ABOUT SARAH

You can't help feeling more than a little enthused, positive and purpose-led once you have spent some time with Sarah Ebanja, the CEO of Tottenham Hotspur (commonly known as Spurs) Foundation. The football club is now the proud owner of a state-of-the-art, billion-pound stadium, with a first team playing both Premier League and Champions League football.

Whenever we meet Sarah it is obvious that her unique blend of infectious optimism, steely determination and humility are just what a global and iconic brand needs to leverage in order to maximise the important work of serving and supporting the communities within which Tottenham Hotspur operates. These communities are predominantly in north east London, with some of the neighbourhoods classified as the most deprived in the United Kingdom, a fact Sarah embraces in the knowledge of just how much positive impact can be achieved.

We arranged to meet Sarah near London Bridge station on a summer morning in London which had dawned rather unseasonably wet and windy. Sarah arrived wearing her Tottenham Hotspur emblazoned wind jacket, which we always joke with her, is ironic as we know she is a lifelong Arsenal (Gunners) fan.

Sarah was born in London to a white British mother and a black Cameroonian father, with a brother two years older than herself. Growing up in the countryside of Oxfordshire, she first became conscious of colour from 'a name calling perceptive' as a child and for continually being asked, "Where are you from?" up until the age of 21 (when she moved back to London). However, given her resilient character coupled with a strong supportive family unit, this did not detract Sarah from achieving her goals and aspirations. She cherished the freedom her mother gave her to do whatever she wanted to do in life and so, she did, with a strong sense of not letting prejudice or stereotyping stop her. Instead, Sarah says she focused on the fact that "We are all human beings, and nothing should stifle what we want to do."

Sarah won't describe herself as academic, but she is good at what interests her. She was clearly interested in numbers, having become a certified accountant. Being an accountant provided Sarah a valuable lesson for her career: "All you have to do is follow the money," she told us. "That will really tell you what people (organizations) are focused on." This, in turn, encouraged Sarah to always look for the evidence beyond the mere proposition throughout her business career.

Sarah's career started in taxation and developed into wider corporate management. She has worked in the private sector and public sector, holding a variety of senior positions within local and regional government. The key tenets of Sarah's style and approach are:

- To take accountability for her own decisions and, in so doing, to be comfortable with the potential outcomes of those decisions
- To build resilience, both personally and professionally and to break or undermine stereotypes
- To influence at all levels with humility, while approaching complex tasks with simplicity and always having the end in mind
- To have a clear focus (strategy) with an ability to say 'no' when necessary
- To empower others so that they feel included, with clear context, choice and accountability

- To recognise her personal motivation (purpose) for success in all aspects of her life

Sarah has always gravitated toward working in very purpose-, people- and community-led roles. In addition to 13 years in regional and local government she has held numerous board positions such as the Steven Lawrence Charitable Trust, Leadership Through Sport & Business, the Amos Bursary, Newlon Housing Trust, Capital City College Group and the Royal Society for the encouragement of Arts, Manufactures and Commerce, to name a few. These boards all have something in common as they enable Sarah to contribute to physical and socio-economic betterment of poorer neighbourhoods and to expose and grow individuals' and communities' talent and potential that might otherwise be neglected. "I'm mindful from my own experience that drives me to take on other people's pigeon-holing and tackle others' attitude towards those who grow up in impoverished areas and people of colour. It's just who I am."

We asked, "How have some of the challenges you faced shaped your outlook?" She paused briefly and then responded. "Ethnicity and colour become relevant when viewed against the norm, depending on where you are. Others define you by it based on their own circumstances, norms or 'majority'. It's all relative. When I go to the Caribbean I am labelled 'red'; in South Africa I am "coloured'; in Cameroon I've been referred to as 'white' and in America I am called 'yellow.'" *(This is with reference to the One Drop Rule which was a social and legal principle of racial classification that was historically prominent in the United States in the 20th Century. It asserted that any person with even one ancestor of sub-Saharan African ancestry, i.e. 'one drop' of black blood, was considered black.)* Sarah continued to tell us about the labels in the UK that she has grown up with and been required to identify with. These range from 'half caste' and 'mixed-race' to 'dual heritage' and 'black'. "How do you deal with all these labels?" we asked. "I am a person of colour relative to where I go, but actually I am just me. So, if you need to label me you can label me however you want, but I am still the same person – always."

Sarah recognises that we all attribute labels and carry prejudices, rarely through mischief, but we stereotype and categorise people to make connections and to try to understand situations facing us. In doing so, however, we all face an inherent danger of getting things wrong. Sarah recognizes her own defence mechanism, which has manifested itself through having to battle prejudice, in that she is often probing in her conversations with people in order to try to understand what judgements they might be making of others' behaviours and others' capabilities due to their own assumptions, stereotypes and prejudices. "Ultimately our destination is in our own hands. We all make choices so let's make sure, particularly for young people, that we can nurture and improve their self-efficacy and confidence. Life is a competition, so young people need to believe in themselves, expose themselves to and grasp opportunities."

"So, what brought you to Spurs Football Club?" we asked. "I genuinely believe in the passion that Tottenham Hotspur has in making a difference to the area that it is in; and that is what persuaded me to pursue the opportunity to become the Foundation's chief executive." She continued, "We create opportunities from elite football to benefit the communities that we serve. This ranges from encouraging anyone and everyone to participate in grassroots football in all its guises. We go on to use this as a platform to inspire children, adolescents and adults – people of all ages – to discover and make the best of their talents and choices, whatever those might be. It's giving people the confidence and courage to self-manage, including from improved physical, mental health and wellbeing perspectives. The Foundation's uniform is our tracksuit; we are not an agency and so it acts like a magnet in creating interest and curiosity as to what we are doing. We attract and sustain participants' interest through developing an ongoing relationship where benefit can be seen and realised."

When you meet people like Sarah you understand just how important an industry football is in this part of London and in many parts of the UK. If you have a chance to visit the wonderful new Spurs football stadium on a matchday, you will be in a place where 3,500 people are at work, with more than 20% of local people being employed by the club.

Our time with Sarah drew to a close, but not before she outlined her general approach to life: "I'm not an island. I am as good as the people and partners I work with. I always look for the connectivity between us all. What I do best, I do with others."

CHAPTER THREE

CONTROL

Destination Belief
Someone or something must always be accountable for success (Control)

Journey behaviours   Journey behaviours

Journey Motivator 1   Journey Motivator 2
The extent to which you believe that   The extent to which you
'conducting from the front' will   believe in allowing others to
achieve your desired outcomes   shape the direction of travel

Directive   Participative

| 8 | 12 |

Henri Fayol's Planning, Leadership, Organization and Control (PLOC) concept has defined management theory since the early 1900s.

The French mining engineer's theory holds that a manager's strength and development can be routinely measured against these four key principles. Quite simply, success or failure is gauged by how effectively a manager has planned, led, organized and controlled.

As one of the key values in this metric, and a prominent factor in our research, with more than 34,428 published references, 'control' is a powerful Destination Belief in all high-ranking individual and teams.

From our study of leaders, we noted that while they all understand the critical importance of control, their attitudes toward it (or Journey Motivators) vary greatly.

Twitter executive Bruce Daisley told us this about control: "It's a really important thing to ensure that we acknowledge survivor bias. If you ask any member of the Spice Girls how they became a pop star, they'll tell you 'work really hard'. What you're missing is that there were another hundred would-be pop stars who started at the same time as them, and worked as hard as them, but didn't become pop stars. So, there is a danger of survivor's bias. You are asking me, the one who perhaps succeeded like the Spice Girls through randomness, through good fortune, how I controlled my own journey. You ask what is the secret? I tell you there is no secret."

Bruce acknowledged that luck was a factor in his professional success. "I was very lucky to be the right place at the right time. And I was probably helped by the fact that I was obsessed with the internet." He said the decisions one makes "probably get you another five, ten percent" along the road to success. "There are some things along the way where I have marginally made my own luck."

THROWING THE CV OUT THE WINDOW

After university Bruce spent six months writing letters for jobs and getting nowhere, until he drew a cartoon CV to replace his conventional-looking one. Because he wanted to get into the record business, he sent the cartoon off to 40 record companies. "I got immediate responses, and people phoning me up, offering a long lunch," he said. "I got a bit of work experience that way."

Bruce said Virgin Records offered him a job as its post boy, "where everyone starts at Virgin Records". He was told that he'd have to drive to the post office every day. But there was a problem.

"I didn't have a driving licence," Bruce said. "So, I said, how about this: I'd taken a crash-course before, and then my test was cancelled on the day it was supposed to happen. How about I take a crash-course and I can take a driving licence test in two weeks? If I pass my driving test, I'll start here the following Monday, but if I don't pass I'll give you the job back."

Going forward, as he saw job adverts in the newspaper, he would redraw the first two squares in his cartoon CV so that it aligned with the employment opportunity. And that led to his first job with Capital Radio, even though his interview went badly. The radio station's management told him so outright. "You were terrible at the interview," Bruce was told. "You seem too shy, and you didn't really know a lot about the job, but everyone in the office – a hundred people in the office – were rooting for you. Everyone was like, 'how did the cartoon boy go?'"

The reaction was so overwhelming that management told him: "We have to give you a job!" In retrospect, Bruce said: "That made me feel: 'Okay, so I did make a bit of luck for myself.' Yeah, but you know, it only has an impact around the edges."

IT DOESN'T
TAKE A HERO

Directive leaders are best characterized by their ability – and desire – to take complete control of a situation. A case in point: General Norman Schwarzkopf, who served as commander of United States Central Command and led all coalition forces in the First Gulf War. Schwartz-kopf famously wrote in his autobiography, *It Doesn't Take a Hero*,[14] that taking control is the best way to lead.

"When placed in command, take charge," Schwartz-kopf wrote, saying that directive leadership simplifies decision-making.

The thinking goes that directive leaders who take defin-itive control make more decisions than those who don't exercise that control. And making decisions, even incorrect ones, has more of a positive impact than doing nothing. A leader who makes hundreds of incorrect decisions, the thinking goes, has more impact than a leader who makes no decisions at all. According to Schwarzkopf, that's because a leader who's made hundreds of incorrect deci-sions has ruled out hundreds of things that do *not* work. And that makes him or her better prepared to take the next leadership step.

Leaders who keenly relate to this Journey Motivator are strong, forthright and confident – sometimes to the point of arrogance. As Schwarzkopf observes: "To be an effec-tive leader, you have to have a manipulative streak. You have to figure out the people working for you and give each tasks that will take advantage of his strength."

Yet, there is a lingering question that can plague the directive leader: Can one person possibly control every outcome for an indefinite period of time?

Participative leaders and managers believe the answer is 'no'. As the boxer Mike Tyson famously said: "Everyone has a plan until they get punched in the mouth." Leaders with a strong affinity for the Participative Journey Motivator conserve their energy and look with open minds at a variety of sources as they make decisions. They lead with the assistance of historical knowledge, patient observation and input from the many voices in the room.

RECOGNIZING THE POWER OF OTHERS

Dr Piet Noë graduated from Belgium's Ghent University as an ophthalmologist. He volunteered to go to Rwanda, where he worked for nine years with a German non-governmental organization at Kabgayi Hospital in the city of Gitarama, now known as Muhanga. During his years there, Piet built an extensive practice treating patients suffering from retinoblastoma, a rare form of eye cancer that occurs almost exclusively in young children.

He eventually used all his savings to purchase a hilltop plot of land. It was there that Piet and his Rwandan associate, Pierre, began constructing a state-of-the-art charity hospital for the many local people suffering from eye conditions.

In order to finance his project, Piet spent time back in Europe, working at the Erasmus University Medical Center in Rotterdam. He returned to Rwanda at the end of 2017. From that time on, Piet was to be the full-time planner, financier, trench digger, inspirational entrepreneur, dedicated medical doctor, visionary and, at times, the lone madman who believed in the art of the possible.

Piet's amazing eye hospital on the hill opened its doors on 18 November 2018, and he has since welcomed patients from all over the region supported by a staff of 42. The search for his third ophthalmologist is now underway. How did it all come to pass? Piet is a participative leader who realized that the power of others was key to overcoming the challenges that had stood in the way of one man and his incredible purpose: to serve.

Typically, by delving into the detail, tweaking and correcting their course in the face of stormy situations, these sorts of leaders have no trouble allowing others to take control in the pursuit of objectives. In an era of constant change, we've observed in our research a growing trend toward a humbler style of leadership. Think of it as 'fellowship' leadership, with individual team members being empowered to lead and thrive, when and where appropriate.

Many may see the term 'able follower' as mildly dismissive, but effective modern-day leaders will blend the need for active control with an ability to morph into able follower in the knowledge that others are at times better placed, experienced or qualified to step forward.

THE LEADER BECOMING A FOLLOWER

The power of a leader becoming an able follower became strikingly apparent on the evening of 16 October 1998, on the cold streets of Kentish Town, north London.

Police had received a report of a domestic incident in which a man had allegedly taken a female hostage. The senior officer on duty was first on the scene, followed by local uniformed officers, a unit of the specialized Territorial Support Group (TSG) and a mobile firearms team. As would routinely be the case, the senior officer stepped forward to assess, direct and lead the police response.

Meanwhile, the local beat officer, who'd also heard the radio alert, arrived on foot moments later. He immediately recognized the address; he'd responded to previous domestic situations there, leading to a string of arrests and court cases. As such, the officer knew both the hostage and the hostage-taker. He was familiar with their family history, their personalities and temperaments, the names of their kids, even what soccer team they supported.

With this new perspective, the senior officer immediately stepped aside, asking the beat officer to let him know what the best course of action would be and what resources he needed. The senior officer was now the able follower: still able to support, but follow he must.

And so, for the next 30 minutes the beat cop sat on the cold concrete and with patience, humility and a new-found dose of authority talked through the letter box with the hostage-taker. He was a troubled 28-year-old man named Steve, and the hostage was his mother. He had threatened her, himself and the officers with a knife he'd been wielding. Yet, following that brief conversation, out came Steve, willingly, calmly and compliantly ... all because the neighbourhood officer had asked him to.

How remarkable. Not only did the beat cop peacefully resolve a volatile episode, but the person in charge helped make it so by quickly recognizing that someone else was better placed, experienced and qualified to step forward.

SHINING THE SPOTLIGHT ON OTHERS

Twitter's Bruce Daisley talks a lot about this. He puts other people ahead of himself, and genuinely enjoys seeing others in the spotlight. He takes steps to make others feel appreciated, valued and significant in the context of his business agenda.

Indeed, he has one of the smallest egos we've ever encountered. He simply doesn't look for or want public praise. Bruce talks openly about not having all the answers, and he has no discernible interest in status. Tellingly, in our relatively short interview, he used the word 'love' 38 times. Here are two examples:

"I just love it when people achieve things and they're able to look at what they've achieved and say, you know, we made that happen. I've worked with bosses who like to claim the credit for everything, and it's exhausting. It's not the truth, and it actually feels incredibly, totally emotionally damaging if someone is trying to claim credit for something they didn't do."

"I love it when they're thinking, 'I can't believe we've just done that.' And you know, my job is to provide the burst of energy, and give them the freedom to do it."

To be the best leader, there has to be a fusion of both Journey Motivators – leading from the front and allowing others to steer the ship. Finding the ratio, and knowing when to prioritize one over the other, is the challenge.

JOURNEY MOTIVATOR 1
CONDUCTING FROM THE FRONT WILL ACHIEVE MY DESIRED OUTCOMES (DIRECTIVE)

Leading from the front is not easy. Winding through dark tunnels, hoisting the lamp over your head as others follow blindly behind clinging to your coattails, trusting you to tell them where to put their feet, at what pace, all while struggling to not fall flat on your face. Directive leaders shoulder enormous responsibility for results and outcomes.

Such a burden doesn't typically allow for debate over how to get to the destination. Leaders empowered by this Journey Motivator take on a singular approach: one leader, many followers.

High performers with a strong affinity for this Journey Motivator have traditionally exercised directive leadership in times of great change, for instance, when a company faces rapid expansion, or at its lowest point of morale.

Bruce Daisley told us that he doesn't believe in sugar-coating his communication, artificially prefacing the message with positivity or taking the easy option of 'leadership avoidance'. While those who don't know him well may find this a bit uncomfortable, they soon come to trust him and recognize that he is never unkind in the way he engages. He avoids ambiguity and accelerates understanding. He deals in facts rather than opinions and expects others to apply rationality to their argument.

"People know that I am very directly honest, so if I say something it's often not sugar-coated for good or for ill,"

Bruce said. "Yeah, they know that if I say something, I'll often say it quite bluntly, and I won't try and start by saying three nice things and then something blunt. I'm pretty direct, and some people find that hard to deal with."

Yet, he finds that most people don't seem to have a problem with his style, because he tries not to be unkind and the last thing he wants is to create a commotion. "People pretty much always know where they stand with me," he said. "They know they're going to get the unvarnished truth. I'm not going to say something that's easy for me to say. I've got urgency to a lot of what I want to do, but I'm also very aware that when you have a business like ours, if you're impatient to grab audience that impatience is actually going to be damaging. Because, for example, it makes you seek out convenient and simplistic answers."

CONTEXT AND UNDERSTANDING

Jaguar Land Rover's Chris Newitt shares a similar philosophy. "I genuinely believe in being as open and honest as you possibly can with your team, because knowledge is power," he told us. "I believe that if I provide my team with the broadest context and broadest understanding of whatever is happening within the business at the time, they'll do their job better. They can rationalize it in their own minds within the context, make better decisions and operate at a higher level."

One of the best examples of a leader who has achieved extraordinary, sustained results across diverse markets and geographies is Sir Richard Branson. He believes in collaboration, respect and fairness, and at the same time he can be fast, decisive, brave and entrepreneurial. The title of one of his best-read books says it all: *Screw It, Let's Do It*.

As Sir Richard tells the story, in 1977 the 28-year-old record store entrepreneur was on his way to the British Virgin Islands to rendezvous with a young lady. When his connecting flight out of Puerto Rico was cancelled, he chartered a plane for £2,000 and – in a gambit to lure other stranded passengers into sharing the cost – he wrote on a blackboard, 'Virgin Airlines – One way flight to Virgin Islands, £39'. He acted boldly ... and with that, one of the world's most successful airlines was born. In 2018 Virgin Atlantic Airways reported revenues of £2.8 billion.

Simply go forth and conquer, they will say. True, these leaders have their place, and they can make a tremendous impact. Yet the fact remains that these sorts of leaders usually have to hand the reins over to someone else when the crisis, challenge or hurdle is overcome. The notion of legacy is not usually associated with a shoot-from-the-hip type of leader.

Here is a short list of the directive leader's most frequently observed behaviours:

1. Powerful/dominating
2. Self-confident/courageous
3. Decisive/wilful
4. Confrontational/challenging
5. Self-sufficient

ENGAGED IN LEADERSHIP ALL ALONG

Conducting from the front to achieve desired outcomes means something very specific for renowned brain surgeon Peter Lees, one of the Iconics we introduced earlier. "Do good doctors lead, or do they manage their patients?" we asked, sitting in his office. "There is evidence that doctors like the term 'leadership', and certainly prefer it to 'management', because leadership holds a certain mystique,"

Peter said. "That's unhelpful, as it may be interpreted as a skill with which only the selected few are born. But if you ask any group of doctors under the age of 30 if they are leaders – you will only need the fingers of one hand to count! They don't believe that *they* are leaders. But all of us have been engaged in leadership since we were toddlers – it's just that we didn't call it that. In any group interaction, leadership emerges in some form or other. Leadership is simply about achieving things 'with and through people'. End of mystique!"

In fact, the number of doctors in management positions in the UK is declining. A study published by the management consultants McKinsey & Company with the London School of Economics found that in 2009 just 58% of NHS managers had any sort of clinical degree, compared with 64% in France, 71% in Germany, 74% in the US and 93% in Sweden.[15] Yet, there is evidence that clinically qualified managers improve performance.

Amanda H. Goodall, of Germany's Institute of Labor Economics (IZA), found a strong positive association between the quality of US hospitals and whether the chief executive was a physician. International research conducted by McKinsey in 2011[16] found that a higher proportion of clinically qualified managers tends to improve the quality of management, and better management improves patient outcomes, such as mortality rates. The research suggested that clinical training gave managers a better understanding of the processes of care delivery, made it easier for them to communicate with clinical staff and gave them greater credibility.

Research by the Health Research and Educational Trust in the US[17] points to a trend toward developing clinician managers through new roles – such as Vice President (VP) of clinical transformation, VP of medical management and VP of clinical informatics – which are being filled by doctors as hospitals give clinicians leading roles in reorganizing care delivery.

The rewards are high for healthcare chief executives in the US. The Harvard School of Public Health found that the average salary for a CEO of an American non-profit hospital is around $600,000 (£480,000; €540,000), and salaries over $1 million are unexceptional.[18] Data from the American College of Healthcare Executives in 2006 showed that chief executives were in their posts for an average of 5.6 years.[19]

As we've described, directive leaders recognize the benefits of a dominant approach. In certain situations, conducting from the front will achieve desired outcomes, such as initiating a project, giving responsibilities to direct reports to complete it and applying specific standards to the quality of work being completed.

These directive leaders set deadlines, define tasks and enforce firm rules and boundaries; they invariably focus on their own experiences and opinions above those of others. They set the direction of the vision and the mission. That means their direct reports may not be required (or encouraged) to offer suggestions or provide feedback to the leader. Their work performance can be judged solely by how well they're performing their assigned tasks. As such, directive leaders must know how to complete a project.

Along the way, these leaders must have confidence in their ability to communicate this information to others without appearing to be arrogant. They must also be able to recognize when someone is resisting their control, in order to reduce delays or address drops in productivity.

THE PACE-SETTING LEADER

Directive leaders in our study were most effective when their experience and knowledge was used to implement specific structures for others. When a team is inexperienced with the duties a project requires, this leadership style can step in. The leader will implement specific tasks and set the pace, in a manner that's been explored by author and science journalist Daniel Goleman. As Goleman described it, the experience of 'the pace-setting leader' can be transferred to each worker, facilitating a positive outcome.

As such, this Journey Motivator emphasizes safety and security; rules and regulations are the primary emphasis of the directive leadership style. Workers are asked to perform tasks in a certain way, for specific reasons, creating clarity within role expectations. Those who have a directive leader are not left questioning what their assignment will be; the leader will present concise expectations. Enforcement of these expectations is often done through rewards and consequences, which can lower the stress levels of workers who try to avoid creative job functions. This clarity often leads to improved performance levels for a team as well.

One way that master chef John Campbell achieves this is through constant questions. "On a day-to-day basis I'll walk the coal face, trying to gather a flavour of the business," John told us. "I'll ask somebody: What's dinner today? How is everybody? How are our suppliers? And it's really just asking questions, not me 'checking'. What's the mood in the camp? What do I need to do? Are we going to coach, or leave it as it is?"

During our research for this book we spent time with over 200 recent-graduate police officers. They were in the first two weeks of their on-the-job training and soon to be deployed across England's 43 national police forces. Their experienced facilitator team was a blend of police, civilian and specialist personnel, from various criminal justice functions and agencies. The young recruits' collective enthusiasm was palpable, and while initial training was directive, structured and controlling, it was also highly supportive of their desire to have a positive impact as serving police officers.

PRIMING THE TALENT PIPELINE

Businesses too are learning how to strike a balance between direction and empowerment for the young, 21st century workforce coming through their talent pipelines. "Feed the passion and let them fly," said one of the police facilitators.

But where does this leave us in terms of freedom and flexibility? Should we all aspire to be titans of directive leadership, like Donald Trump or Larry Ellison? No!

Remember, a high-performing leader demonstrates an optimal balance of two opposing Journey Motivators. Out of an allocation of 20 points (the process explained in Chapter 1) the highest performers were assessed as having a balance of 8 points for directive control and 12 points for participative control.

What does this mean? In layman's terms, they are both directive and participative, though the key to success is learning when to adopt which approach. And this is what they do more effectively than lower-performing leaders; this is the difference that makes the difference.

JOURNEY MOTIVATOR 2
I BELIEVE IN ALLOWING OTHERS TO SHAPE THE DIRECTION OF TRAVEL (PARTICIPATIVE)

"All for one, and one for all!" proclaims the participative leader. More conversation facilitators than generals charging into battle, leaders with this Journey Motivator strive to empower others to contribute to and execute strategy.

When considering the Participative Journey Motivator, Bruce Daisley told us: "Strategy is just the plan for how you're going to do something. The objective is where you're going, and the strategies are the route you're going to take to get there. I see myself as a router – my job is to let information come in, and I choose where to direct my energy. I haven't got opinions or answers on a lot of things, but I just try to help direct energy."

At their best, participative leaders are experts at two-way communication, providing and receiving constant feedback, having one-on-one meetings and exchanges with stakeholders. They possess a gift for adapting their management styles to different types of people, with differing levels of ability, and foster an inclusive, open approach to decision-making. They are usually mentors and guides for individuals and teams around them.

As James Knight told us: "When it comes to leadership command roles, I feel like it's a series of lessons that you've got wrong. That's how you grow and develop as a commander or leader."

UNLIMITED CAPACITY FOR IMPROVEMENT

James continued: "I always put more time and effort and energy into understanding the people under my command, and what really motivates, inspires or interests them. Their capacity for improvement is just limitless. The number one thing is being a good listener. I also like the word 'empathy' when I think of command, so people understand what it's like for everyone else underneath them. If you have a personal agenda, it comes across very strongly; if your agenda is for the benefit of the team, that comes across very strongly. And I know which camp I'd rather be in."

The major caveat to participative leadership lies in the element that makes directive leadership so powerful: time. Operating in a VUCA world, where time is often limited, how do you slow down in order to make better-formed leadership decisions?

Colonel John Boyd addressed that question relative to the life-and-death challenges facing jet-fighter pilots engaged in aerial warfare. Boyd enlisted in the US Army Air Corps as a teenager, in late World War II, and went on to become a Korean War fighter pilot, Vietnam-era commander and respected military strategist. He devised the 'OODA loop' decision cycle, which calls for one to Observe, Orient, Decide and Act in response to an event – and to do so more quickly than an opponent.

In a dogfight, a pilot must observe the enemy as things move at incredible speed. They have to orient their position, consider what options are available, assess the risks and calibrate how it all fits into the broader battle objectives. Based on this orientation, they make a decision and take action. In a typical dogfight a pilot may go through a dozen loops, and through this systematic process they'll benefit from the aggregation of marginal gains and – hopefully – stay a step ahead of the enemy. Speed is not the decisive differentiator; the effectiveness of decision-making is the difference that makes the difference.

In the world of sport there are many examples of slowing down in order to speed up. Analysts who have studied international tennis champion Novak Djokovic observed that he takes several milliseconds longer than his rival in deciding how to play a shot. This time gives him a greater ability to observe his opponent, the ball and the environment, affording him more time to make decisions and execute his shot. These marginal gains have helped make him the best tennis player in the world.

From a business perspective, one of the best examples of this thinking is Warren Buffet. The legendary CEO, investor and philanthropist leads the 390,000-employee conglomerate Berkshire Hathaway and is one of the world's wealthiest people. "I insist on a lot of time being spent, almost every day, to just sit and think," he said. "That is very uncommon in American business. I read and think. So, I do more reading and thinking, and make fewer impulsive decisions than most people in business."

'UNSTICKING' THE ORGANIZATION

Duke CE, in researching its 2019 *Shift White Paper*,[20] spoke to a number of executives on the issue of time. They explored how many equate it with speed, which in turn they relate to decision velocity. An accelerating pace of change requires an accelerated pace of strategic evolution.

A common concern among the CEOs interviewed was how to 'unstick' their organizations from outdated internal structures and chains of command that impede swift decision-making. Instead, they sought to imbue all levels of leadership with a greater sense of urgency.

There was a consensus among these executives that organizations are not moving fast enough, and that they're often burdened by past practices that, while familiar and convenient, lack the agility and responsiveness required in today's complex, ever-changing environment. At the same time, the CEOs were especially concerned about how regional factors like politics, economics and competitors were impacting their ability to adapt ... not just quickly, but effectively.

In participant leadership, the leader turns to the team for input, ideas and observations instead of making all the decisions on his or her own. That's not to say the leader doesn't have the ultimate decision-making responsibility, but it's tempered by an understanding that the team may have skills and ideas that could benefit the decision-making process.

Michael Tobin, one of our Iconics, said: "As a young leader I was super green. I thought leadership was shouting louder than everyone else. I didn't understand what leadership was – I thought it was management and I was scared. So, I wouldn't invite people in who were better than me. I wouldn't allow them freedom; I wanted to be the centre of attention. It was my way or the highway. Now that I'm way more experienced, I'm not embarrassed about not knowing something. My value is to surround myself with clever people and mostly ask questions."

Participant leadership involves the entire team. This is a style in which the leader works closely with team members, focusing on building relationships and rapport. On the flip side of this leadership coin you have the autocratic leadership style, in which the leader tends to be more issue-focused and makes most decisions without input from the team.

It's a style we saw work especially well in a time-critical environment, such as policing, military and crisis experiences.

One example shared by James Knight really stood out for us. "I was very keen that all of my company headquarters treated everyone like an adult," he said. "We arrived in Manchester, and we were all going out for beers. And so rather than give them a curfew and telling them all the penalties if you get it wrong and focus on the negatives, I just said that as the bus leaves at 10 o'clock tomorrow – you're either on it or not. We had a great night, and sure enough every single person was on."

ASSISTED DECISION-MAKING

Why does participant leadership work well in certain situations? Allowing the team to assist in the decision-making process, to give input and to share ideas, increases the team's involvement as a whole. When the leader says to the team, "I trust you to help me work on this problem and reach a solution," those being entrusted by the leader feel empowered. They feel that their skills are being acknowledged and their opinions are being valued. Team members feel that they add worth to the company when the leader is asking for input and listening to suggestions.

Another participant leadership trait mentioned by James can be particularly effective. "I once saw a senior officer come in and meet us for the first time," he said. "He began by telling us what he was really bad at. I thought, wow, that's impressive. All he's done is tell us what he's weak at, what his insecurities are. So, I learned to do the same. I am impatient, and I'm impulsive, and I tell my team exactly that. I immediately highlight what my weaknesses are."

Participative leadership brings a wide range of ideas and potential solutions to the table as organizations work through problems. Having a team of people considering options for marketing a new product, for instance, introduces countless ideas that might not have surfaced had the leader been inclined to do the all thinking and make the final decision with no additional input.

Peter Lees had this perspective: "I like to know 10% of absolutely everything, and then understand how that looks relative to the bigger picture, because I'm fully aware that some people can't join the dots between various scenarios. I think, actually, I'm kind of okay with that."

Those who were excellent participant leaders also typically showed a willingness to speak last during meetings, ensuring that all others had voiced their views and opinions. On many occasions the confidence to listen, and speak last, gave the leader the ultimate platform of knowledge, options and oversight before they contributed. Some described this as 'a leader's curiosity'.

The issue of curiosity was touched on in the Duke CE 2018 *What's Next in Leadership* paper.[21] Is curiosity a positive by-product of participant leadership? If so, it harnesses time, patience, humility, listening skills and 'questioning the obvious', to name a few potent attributes. Participant leaders have a well-developed sense of curiosity. This can help them embrace diversity; unlearn bad habits; learn new skills; dedicate more time for creativity; develop flexibility in listening; view work through multiple lenses; remain open-minded; and commit to lifelong learning and rigorous experimentation. To become less rigid and more curious, many senior leaders simply need to learn to 'let go.'

A GROWTH MINDSET

The participative leader also fosters a growth mindset, which opens the door to myriad possibilities. Curiosity must not be underestimated. Duke CE's paper suggested a simple, six-point plan for fostering curiosity.

1. Continually ask 'why' rather than clinging to what you already know. Leaders have traditionally been rewarded and promoted for having answers and knowing with some certainty what to do in any given situation. In many cases leaders place that expectation on themselves. The accelerating pace of change means that it's unrealistic, and sometimes dangerous, to continue playing the 'expert' – one who's seen it all before and always knows the best course of action. Data is so abundant that it's difficult to filter the noise from the meaning. On the other hand, new issues arise for which there is little empirical evidence to guide your decisions. Rather than maintaining hierarchy and control, strive to embrace the uncertainty with curiosity.

2. Challenge the status quo. Learning to adapt is a minimum requirement. Developing curiosity requires going further and deeper – an insatiable quest to test assumptions, like long-standing policies and practices. Curious people want to know why things are the way they are, what motivates individuals and groups to act as they do and what trends in the external environment may affect your business. They look for potential and they experiment. In short, they get excited about possibilities and frequently ask, 'How might we …' to test novel ideas and new approaches.

3. Acknowledge biases. We are born curious, as we have no experience to guide or filter our thinking, but we can also develop the skill. As we grow and learn we start to develop mental models and expectations as to how things work. Unfortunately, as our knowledge and expertise deepens, this abiding sense of curiosity often declines. Leaders can re-awaken that curious mind by being aware of and working to minimize their biases.

4. Engage in personal introspection. This happens by considering questions like:
   - What am I feeling?
   - Why?
   - How did my behaviour impact others?
   - What did I miss?
   - What could I be doing differently?

   This practice also helps in developing humility and self-awareness.

5. Consciously develop inquiry and critical thinking skills. Leaders must nurture what Zen masters call 'a beginner's mindset' to free themselves from habitual, automatic or default thinking. This is in fact the opposite of the 'leader as expert' model that dominates so much of business today. A Zen master sums up the benefits of curiosity nicely: "In the beginner's mind, there are many possibilities. In the expert's mind, there are few."

6. Be courageous and resilient. (Resilience is dealt with in the next chapter.) It's not easy to question your own thinking, and even harder to challenge corporate orthodoxies. Some colleagues will be defensive, others will be resistant and some may be outright defiant. Leaders need to expect and be well prepared for any of these reactions. The curious mindset will be beneficial even in the face of these challenges and curiosity will help leaders uncover the 'why' behind others' reaction to change.

However, participant leadership should not be confused with laissez-faire leadership. In this scenario, the leader gives the power of decision-making to the group, along with the materials needed to make the decision. While this style might work in certain situations – such as when a decision must be made about something the leader is not familiar with – in many instances participant leadership simply works better. There is a fine line between a laissez-faire approach and flat-out abdication of accountability.

When a leader apportions control to the team, they must ensure that every step to a successful outcome is clearly mapped and explained, with regular meetings and other forms of formal communication. As Chris Newitt says: "There is the battle between permanent meetings and creating time to do stuff, and to think and reflect. You have to be selfish, which for me involves potentially working from home or trying to gain some form of external stimulus, in whatever form that might be."

This requires drawn-out and often informal discussions to get to the detail of the problem and arrive at a plan of action. The 'buy-in' of the team must be a priority if this type of leadership is to succeed. This can only be achieved if the work is under no serious time constraints.

TOGGLING BETWEEN PASSIVE AND PROACTIVE

Some of those we spoke with remembered their own challenge of moving between the passive and the proactive. Tamara Rojo told us that as a dancer she had a "passive role, responding to what task was given, or what I was told to do. As a leader it is the opposite. I have to lead the way, show direction, take risks and initiatives and persuade others."

The Participative Journey Motivator ensures that a team is in the best possible shape at the end of its journey. Still, deadlines and goals may be missed if they aren't mapped out and measured in good time throughout the process.

It also requires trust in the team and its collective effort, which is an altogether different kind of motivational challenge for the leader. Michael Tobin put it this way: "I work with people based on trust. They can always learn how to do the job and learn a new skill set, but I can't teach them trust."

The most frequently observed behaviours and characteristics among participant leaders include:

- Team player/generous with time and knowledge
- People pleasing
- Caring
- Dependent on others
- Easily distracted and scattered

So, what is the key difference between high- and lower-performing leaders? Both seem to value participant leadership more highly than its directive counterpart. And while this is true, lower-performing leaders seem less able (or willing) to use directive leadership when the situation requires it.

Participative leadership tends to work best when you aren't making decisions 'under fire', which in today's VUCA world is rare. When time is of the essence and a decision needs to be made, this style can be problematic. You can't always call an on-the-spot meeting to figure out the solution to a problem. Such leadership isn't always successful in situations where team members don't have access to the end goals, or when they lack the skills needed to create solutions to specific problems. This might be true if the leader is in a position that required specialized training that the rest of the team didn't receive, or when decisions are based on classified information that can't be shared.

Ultimately, it is in these moments of difficulty that great leaders will emerge. In the moment of truth, they'll use the right style, whether it be directive or participative. Heroes are made in moments of self-doubt. Michael Tobin talks a lot about this. "I like deals that people think are not easy to do, or people think are impossible to do," he said.

LEADING UNDER EXTRAORDINARY CIRCUMSTANCES

In Rwanda we witnessed first-hand the power of using the right leadership style in an extraordinary set of circumstances.

We worked with the team at Duke CE assisting a leading pharmaceutical client who has for some six years worked with local healthcare teams in Kigali, the nation's capital, and rural villages in northern Rwanda. Their focus is on epilepsy, a chronic central nervous system condition that causes recurrent seizures, sparked by abnormal electrical activity in the brain. Symptoms may vary, and in many cases the cause is unknown.

Now, place this medical condition in the most remote, rural villages of central Africa. Some villagers believe

CHAPTER THREE
CONTROL

that the disorder is a result of either witchcraft or family curses, or that it is contagious. Persons living with epilepsy are therefore hidden away, or in extreme cases they're literally beaten as part of a traditional curing process. Now imagine suffering an epileptic fit some 10 kilometres from the nearest medical centre, which you'd need to walk to through difficult hilly terrain. Compounding these difficulties is a profound distrust of outsiders and modern medicine.

Enter Dirk Teuwen, VP of Corporate Societal Responsibility for Union Chimique Belge and Dr Fidèle Sebera, a neurologist at the CARAES Neuropsychiatric Hospital with Rwanda's Ministry of Health. Fidèle and Dirk have been working together to treat people living with epilepsy and offer access to diagnosis and treatment. Fidèle has been for more than 10 years the only neurologist in Rwanda. Their work has significantly improved the lives of these people and their families.

This medical team quickly realized a directive approach to treating epilepsy was not enough to overcome the significant educational and many trust barriers that are pervasive in Rwanda's rural villages. However, help was to come from an unlikely source – the head of the district's traditional healers.

Why would modern medical practitioners spend time with traditional healers? How do you reconcile modern medicine with historic tradition that relies on remedies like ritual beatings or plant concoctions? Why would you even try? In this case, it was because the district's senior faith healer, Mr Innocent Hitimana, holding sway over a network of 500 traditional healers, was willing to explore. If traditional healers could be convinced of the doctors' good intent, and the benefits of the latest epilepsy treatments, could they credibly spread the word among villagers?

Quite unexpectedly, while travelling with Dirk and Fidèle, we came to witness the first-ever meeting between Innocent, head of the traditional healers and Dr Fidèle, the neurologist. The chance meeting occurred in the back-yard of Innocent's home, with his wife Languide and some of their children present. Now was not the time for direc-tive leadership – the situation clearly called for participant leadership, with an abundance of curiosity, unlearning and humility.

AN EXERCISE IN CURIOSITY, DEFERENCE AND LISTENING

There we all sat, in Innocent's backyard, where, apart from bits of sketchy translation, we had nothing more than observation, voice intonation, body language and at times excited emotional hand gestures to help us figure out how this unusual meeting was progressing. The tra-ditional healer involved his wife throughout and the kids were fascinated by the three white men who'd appeared unexpectedly in their backyard as they tried to play. This was truly an exercise in acute curiosity, deference, listening and participant leadership. The stakes were high.

Each side took turns speaking, listening, asking ques-tions and explaining. Bridging a long-standing divide, facing an unusual and acute uncomfortableness in willing an impossible to become possible, accepting an acceler-ated unlearning of established education and culture and becoming united in a prospect of bringing, jointly, a better health to underprivileged patients. After some time, they earned a handshake on a collaboration in the best interests of hundreds, if not thousands, of people living with epilepsy in the far-flung villages of Rwanda. Throughout, Fidèle and Dirk stayed close to their 3H principles: humility, honesty and health.

Great leaders simply refuse to accept that their success is based on fate or circumstance. To them, success is a choice. Choosing to keep going when barriers are put up all around you can be daunting or discouraging. Challenges seem insurmountable and everyone seems determined to weaken your resolve. At times like this, the decision to carry on is what heroes are made of. That resolve – together with accepting that one person can't do it all on their own – is key to becoming a successful leader. Those are the leaders who leave behind a legacy that will lift up, energize and inspire others. Time will tell, and Dirk and Fidèle, along with the traditional healers of the different remote villages may, through their persistence and leadership, be about to positively change the lives of thousands of children and adults living with epilepsy and their loved ones.

A number of CEOs we spoke with said that if they sometimes needed to act in a directive manner – perhaps during times of volatile change or crisis – they also worked hard to avoid a 'hero culture' where one person was viewed as the saviour or ultimate problem-solver. They then shifted from directive to participant leadership in order to manage the events, but also to quickly empower others going forward.

James Knight echoed that sentiment when we spoke with him: "Let go of a responsibility to the point where it starts to feel uncomfortable, and then you'll know that you're getting it right. When I was in the jungle a couple years ago, my second-in-command was kind of doing the nuts and bolts organizing of it. And in the end, I didn't attend the evening meeting, and he ran it on his own, which kind of put me in this awkward position where I had almost nothing to do. But he ran this whole exercise, and it ran really well. I'd removed myself, and we would speak every night anyway, but it felt uncomfortable. But perhaps that was the point where I was getting it right."

MY CONTROL REVIEW

Below are some questions relating to the Destination Belief of Control. Find a quiet place, contemplate the questions and write down your responses. Better still, verbalize them out loud. Doing so will move you along on the journey of applying The Leader's Secret Code.

Q1. When something doesn't go as planned, who has final accountability?

Q2. Do other people's ideas have value to you? If so, why is that?

Q3. How do you think stakeholders feel when they are allowed to contribute to your decision-making?

Q4. How do you cope if a team or project you are leading fails?

Q5. Who are your role models?

WHAT'S IN THE MIND?

The psychologist says ...

This Destination Belief reads that something or someone must always be accountable for success (control); in any situation, in any circumstance while embracing any extraneous variables (things you cannot control but which have an effect). With such variations in any given situation, leadership cannot be viewed as black or white. Each leader is different, as is their leadership style, as will be the outcome.

In 2000, Daniel Goleman, world-renowned leadership and EQ expert, researched over 3,000 executives to extract what it is effective leaders do. From this research, Goleman not only wanted to establish what it was that leaders do, but also the effect this would have on the organization and their people. Goleman created the Six Leadership Styles[22] and found, in his research, that leaders used one of these styles at any one time. Each of the Six Leadership Styles comes from the use of EQ: how a leader manages their personality to be both personally and interpersonally effective.

Let's explore two of the leadership styles from Goleman's work: Commanding versus Affiliative. A commanding leadership style could be described as 'do it because I say so' with the objective of immediate compliance from the individual. This relates to the Journey Motivator of Directive; the extent to which you believe that 'conducting from the front' will achieve your desired outcomes. Within this style, the leaders rarely seeks any input from others, controls tightly through constant monitoring, motivates others but emphasising the consequences of getting it wrong and often relies on negative, corrective feedback to others.

This style can be most effective when dealing with relatively straightforward tasks and in crisis situations where individuals need clear direction and the leader has more information that the individuals involved. Where this style is most ineffective is:

- When dealing with a complex situation
- Working with highly competent individuals
- Over a longer-term timeframe because individuals who are not being developed or listened to may tire, rebel or leave.

The Affilitative leadership style holds a primary purpose of creating harmony among individuals and with leaders and individuals. This style of leadership will take an approach of 'People first, task second', cares for the whole person and will share their emotional challenges with team members. Aligning neatly with the Journey Motivator of Participative, 'the extent to which you believe in allowing others to shape the direction of travel', this style is most effective when the individual requires one-to-one assistance in both their personal or professional life, where a leader seeks harmony between conflicting parties or individuals and when recovering trust within a team. This style of leadership becomes ineffective when:

- The leader lacks empathy in situations where they need to relate to the feelings, needs or perspectives of others
- Corrective feedback is required
- In crisis situations, when the leader is required to set direction and ensure it is taken
- Used alone (not in conjunction with another leadership style).

The other four leadership styles are:

- **Pace Setting**: 'Do it my way' while accomplishing tasks to high standards of excellence
- **Visionary**: 'Let's remind ourselves of the bigger purpose', inspiring others with long-term vision and direction
- **Coaching**: 'Let me help you develop' with a strong focus on the development at an individual level
- **Democratic**: 'Let's work it out together', building commitment and idea generation.

The most effective leaders skilfully switch between all six leadership styles based on their assessment of the situation, considering the individuals involved, the environment and the desired outcome. When a leader leads consistently with one style, this can have a negative impact on the individuals and teams they lead. The least positive impact comes from a leadership style of 'over commanding'. When used outside of a crisis it creates medium-term resistance and may seriously damage the organization. In order to use this style most effectively, ask yourself the following questions:

- How does it feel to be led by you? Ask others who are in this position. Listen to their answers.
- How do you wish to be led?
- Have you asked for the opinions of other people and shown a genuine interest in their answers? Reserve the right to make your own decisions but make sure that you've given real attention and consideration to people who hold different views to your own, listening and taking on board their feedback.

- How are you are contributing to this perceived situation? Are you leading by the view that you are the only one who knows how to do things around here? Learn to listen properly; that means being fully present and not just waiting for them to finish speaking so that you can talk again.

THE LAST WORD
ON CONTROL
A LIFE-AFFIRMING LESSON
IN PARTICIPATION

On 5 August 2010 disaster befell the San José copper mine, Chile. A rock the size of a 45-storey building gave way within the mine and started a chain reaction which left 33 miners entombed 700 metres below ground, with at least three quarters of a million tonnes of rock between them and the open air. If the challenge of extracting the men was not great enough, two days into the rescue operation an air shaft gave way, thus cutting off even this potential route out. The Chilean president, Sebastián Piñera, stepped forward from the outset. At this moment what the anxious country needed was a figurehead who could bring people together as never before. Piñera also knew that the best chance of a successful rescue would come once others from all over the world were invited to participate in the process. "We were humble enough to ask for help," he is reported to have said afterwards.

Simply locating the miners was a massive challenge, let alone extracting them once they were found. Interestingly, the rescuers split into different groups, each group working on ways to drill effectively towards where everyone believed the miners were trapped. At various points they stopped working in their teams and came together to evaluate progress. In the end, after some hastily arranged experiments with scientific equipment, they were able to take the experience of the different groups and establish that one group seemed to have more accurate measurements. From this collaboration emerged a strategy.

The rescue mission was a 'round the clock' effort. The change-over of shifts, which could have been a moment of potential weakness in the communication chain, became the time when everyone was brought up to date with everything that was going on – continuity of purpose was key. President Piñera, meanwhile, remained the voice of calm optimism.

NASA engineers, together with the Chilean navy and an array of other scientists, designed the FENIX, a small rescue capsule capable of bringing the miners on a 15-minute solo journey to the surface. And so it was on 13 October 2010, over two months after the disaster had begun, the FENIX brought up the first of the miners, while Chile and the world watched in awe at what was unfolding before their eyes.

What is abundantly clear is that a command and control approach would have doomed the miners. No one person, agency or company was capable of delivering the innovation required in the time available. This incident demonstrated, in stark reality, the need for people to participate fully in order to be successful in this situation. Of course, other situations might require a wholly different approach. Such is the variable nature of leadership.

CHAPTER
FOUR

RESILIENCE

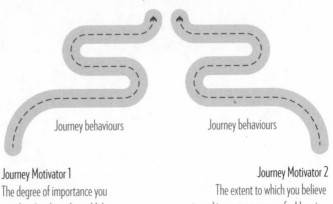

Destination Belief
I am able to withstand tremendous pressure and spring back into shape
(Resilience)

Journey behaviours   Journey behaviours

Journey Motivator 1   Journey Motivator 2
The degree of importance you   The extent to which you believe
attach to 'working through' the   in seeking out new ways of addressing
tough times by raising your   challenges and how to integrate them
level of effort   into your leadership practice

Work Hard   Work Smart

4 **16**

The ability to withstand the slings and arrows of work, life, adversity and failure is crucial for a leader. The ability to dust yourself off and get back on your feet is even more so.

Experts who study stress and resilience believe that our ability to bounce back – and the sense of wellbeing that brings us – comes from the balance of expending energy during performance and taking time for renewal and recovery to regain that burned energy.

A 2018 study found that 80% of US workers "feel stress on the job and nearly half say they need help learning how to manage stress."[23] Added to this, 42% say their co-workers need such help.[24] In the European Union, work-related stress is the second most common occupational health problem, after back pain,[25] affecting 28% of workers. The financial consequences are significant. For example, it is estimated that the cost to European businesses and social security systems adds up to €600 billion a year.[26] In the UK, a 2018 Mental Health Foundation study[27] reported that "74% of people in the previous 12 months have felt so stressed they feel overwhelmed or unable to cope."

Triangulation of these and other available data points from around the world confirms the World Health Organization's assertion that "stress is the global health epidemic of the 21st century."[28]

In the face of this challenge, the question of how individuals and organizations can proactively take action to prevent the onset of stress, instead of reacting to its bad consequences, takes centre stage.

The topic of resilience has received increasing attention from academics and management practitioners in recent years. Much is made in today's management thinking of becoming mentally tough and building resilience in order to deal with a VUCA world.

While evolution has provided human beings with a way to deal with events that can overwhelm us – our capacity to be resilient – our cultural training can override our body's natural instincts for how to maintain mental perspective and physical balance.

KNOWING
WHO YOU ARE

Garret Kramer,[29] whose company specializes in sports psychology, offers a counter-intuitive take on the principles of human experience, as first espoused by the personal-improvement philosopher Sydney Banks.[30] "When you grow tired of seeking resilience or mental toughness, consider this: You'll never find it," Kramer said. "By your nature, you're the opposite of resilient. You're a transient agency of Consciousness. Peace is found in knowing who you are, not in trying to become what you can never be."

Top leaders make resilience a priority, both for their own sake and that of their teams. It's necessary so they can weather the storm, continue making decisions and maintain a healthy lifestyle.

Michael Tobin elaborates on this: "There are two important lessons about working hard and smart. One is learning when to say no and not just following blindly. Know your value and walk away when it's time to walk away. For the second lesson, imagine you're a broom salesman, and from your historical statistics, out of every hundred houses you knock on the door of, 99 of them won't need or want one. Only one of them is not going to have a broom and can afford your broom. So, it doesn't matter where you start on the street, you knock on the door and it's no more or less likely that they'll buy."

Resilience is a natural bedfellow of personal effort, something that 'Everyday Jedi' John Amaechi was very clear on when we met with him.

"Almost every leadership challenge is a function of personal effort and energy expenditure," he told us. "It's not a question of cost to a business, or a question of new structural elements, remuneration or reward: it's just effort." What's also true is that one needs to find multiple sources of personal resilience. As John reminded us: "For any negative experience that you had there is a positive way to learn that lesson. You don't have to be beaten up at school to learn resilience."

You have heard the saying that times of stress 'separate the wheat from the chaff'. The thought is that unwavering, ironclad resilience is what keeps a leader on track during particularly trying times. Without the ability to bounce back from unexpected roadblocks, a leader would flounder and fall flat on their face.

In a VUCA world, with its wild situations and unpredictable circumstances, resilience is a cloak of protection for both leaders and their extended teams. To stay on track in a topsy-turvy world, a company needs its leaders to be as steady as possible as they navigate their people through whatever terrain they encounter.

STRENGTH IN THE FACE
OF HARDSHIP

Much is said and taught about resilience. However, we should never forget the ability of the human spirit to demonstrate fortitude and perseverance in the face of seemingly insurmountable odds. History has provided many examples of those who've found unimaginable strength during unimaginable hardship.

At times, during the research for this book, we simply had to stop and attempt to comprehend how certain forms of resilience were even possible. For an example, we return to Rwanda and our trip to Kigali and the neighbouring villages.

Rwanda is a proud, productive and growing economy, yet it has a brutally dark past. 2019 marks the 25th anniversary of the Rwandan Genocide. At the entrance to the nation's Kigali Genocide Memorial, the word 'Ubumuntu' is displayed. It is related to the South African Zulu word 'Ubuntu' and means 'humanity toward others'. Ubumuntu can be translated as an English phrase: *I am because you are, and you are because I am*. It stands as a symbol of our shared humanity and our interconnectedness.

The slaughter began on 6 April 1994, when members of the majority Hutu population went on a rampage, murdering ethnic Tutsis and those who tried to protect them. The ensuing massacre lasted more than 100 days and claimed the lives of over 800,000 people. The Kigali Genocide Memorial – designed by the architect who created Yad Vashem, Israel's memorial to victims of the Holocaust – stands as a vivid reminder of man's inhumanity to man.

After leaving the memorial we found ourselves incapable of speech for almost 20 minutes as we reflected on the sheer level of brutality that the human species is capable of. And that brings us back us to the matter of resilience. Just three years after the genocide – on the cold, rainy evening of 18 March 1997, in the small town of Nyange, in western Rwanda – students at Saint Joseph's secondary school finished dinner and settled in to study for exams. Suddenly, a group of 'Interahamwe', or *génocidaires*, who'd snuck into the country after a three-year exile in the Democratic Republic of the Congo, attacked the unassuming camp. The security officer was executed and 27 students were pushed into a classroom and forced to separate – Tutsis on one side, Hutus on the other.

In an act of extraordinary defiance and resilience, the students refused to separate themselves. They refused to save their own lives by identifying the differences among them. Instead, the Hutus stood in solidarity with their Tutsi friends.

Chantal Mujawamahoro, a 21-year-old Hutu, was the first to lay down her life for her fellow students. Her name literally means 'maiden of peace'. She bravely stood up to the attackers and proclaimed: "We do not have Hutus or Tutsis here. We are all Rwandans." They shot her in the head, killing her at her desk.

One by one, six more students were assassinated in front of their classmates. Despite the impending slaughter, the young students were determined to stand in unity – undivided in their identity as one. Rather than wasting bullets, the genocidaires rounded up the surviving students and threw grenades into their classroom, leaving them for dead. Most survived, although they were mutilated, many having lost limbs and some blinded.

RESILIENT, DETERMINED, COMMITTED

Today, under President Paul Kagame's government, there are six Rwandan reconciliation villages where survivors and perpetrators live alongside each other. Many do so in the knowledge that they move among those who may well have been responsible for the murder of loved ones. Despite an extraordinarily brutal past, they go forward as a united nation – resilient, determined, committed – working together for a better future.

Resilience is and always will be a complex issue, at times a simply mind-boggling ability. We travelled throughout Rwanda, and while the shadow of the past is ever present, we couldn't help but notice the overwhelming evidence of industriousness, friendship, economic progress and humanity to others.

In general, we found that resilience manifests in leaders as one of two Journey Motivators. There is the idea that pushing oneself harder, demanding perfection and summoning force from deep inside will alone solve a problem. Or, there is the conviction that adversity means an opportunity to find new solutions that will propel a leader and their team forward.

It is also essential that resilient leaders teach this valuable skill to their people, enabling the team to stay on course. Imbued with new-found strength and malleability, they'll be better able to deal with the pressures of the workplace and will perform with greater clarity and purpose. That, in turn, will reduce risk, help protect the company's interests and assets and set the stage for otherwise unattainable levels of success.

JOURNEY MOTIVATOR 1
I 'WORK THROUGH' THE TOUGH TIMES BY RAISING MY LEVEL OF EFFORT (WORK HARD)

Leaders with the Work Hard Journey Motivator are boundless worriers and warriors. In times of stress, these leaders rise to the challenge themselves, attempting to lift obstacles from the path with brute force.

The famous author of the Harry Potter series, J. K. Rowling, knows a lot about resilience. "Rock bottom became the solid foundation on which I rebuilt my life," Rowling said.

The Harry Potter stories were Rowling's escape from reality. When she wrote the first novel, her life was more than problematic. She was going through a divorce and was left to fend for herself and her daughter in a tiny flat in Edinburgh. She was living off government support and her mother had just passed away. After she completed her first book, in 1995, a dozen publishers rejected her. One small publisher even advised her to pursue another line of work entirely, as they didn't believe anything she wrote would be successful.

Through thick and thin, Rowling refused to give up, until eventually – well, the rest is history. "It is impossible to live without failing at something," she said, "unless you live so cautiously that you might as well not have lived at all, in which case you have failed by default."

And it sometimes works ... unless the leader breaks under the weight. For as John Amaechi told us: "Leaders need to realize that to be a great leader – to emanate an environment around you that allows people to deliver optimally – is *energy-expensive*." Many believe they can solve a problem simply by working harder and relentlessly demonstrating a suite of behaviours that supports their cause.

These Work Hard leaders are often described as:

- Persistent
- Strong-willed
- Brave
- Stubborn/immovable
- Easily fatigued over time.

At its worst, this Journey Motivator can cause leaders to insist on their own (and their team's) 100% perfection. With that mindset, time-poor leaders who 'sweat the small stuff' end up failing to act on the most important things and lose sight of the bigger picture altogether.

AN UNSUSTAINABLE APPROACH

Characterized by a 'when the going gets tough, the tough get going' approach – and a tendency to work every hour possible, striving ever onward – this leadership style is simply unsustainable – and top-performing leaders know it. Out of an allocation of 20 points (as explained in Chapter 1) they were assessed as having a Work Hard score of 4 and a Work Smart score of 16.

These findings confirm that working hard is important. However, they value working hard less than they do working smart. They value working smarter to be more effective. That is not to be interpreted as a 'one over the other' proposition, but rather a blended approach in which leaders use working smarter more frequently than working harder.

This idea isn't new. When talking about the difference between smart and hard work it's easy to explain what working hard means. If you want to be successful in the long run, you have to put long hours into your work. You have to start early, before everyone else, and you have to stay up late, when everyone else is away enjoying their evenings.

On the other hand, it's hard to find clear guidelines for what working smart really means and how it's different from hard work. It's obvious that even if you're determined that nobody will outwork you, you'll at some point hit an 'hours worked' ceiling ... and there will always be someone who's willing (and able) to sleep less than you. On top of that, many people work hard, but only a few become truly successful. That's because smart work is what makes the difference.

A leader can be first into the office every morning and last out at night. They can work until their eyes blur and their fingers bleed. But what these behaviours really say is that things are not under control – this leader is disorganized and heading straight into the oncoming headlights of burnout.

Leaders demonstrating this attitude also need to realize that they are the ultimate 'culture carrier' and that their behaviour will be mirrored. It will spread like an infection across their teams, creating a suboptimal – and ultimately unhealthy – working environment.

As such, Work Hard leaders may give themselves permission to rest, replenish and recharge. They could benefit from taking the time to 'pace and plan'. Along the way they may become their own champion, build resilience and manage to ace challenges without falling to pieces.

As Chris Newitt said: "If you're going to have some form of work-life balance, there is a requirement for a level of intellectual horsepower, as much as anything else, just to process the data and to have a filing cabinet that is big enough. That allows you to step away and have a personal life, because of the amount of data that flows through."

JOURNEY MOTIVATOR 2
I BELIEVE IN SEEKING OUT NEW WAYS OF ADDRESSING CHALLENGES AND HOW TO INTEGRATE THEM INTO MY LEADERSHIP PRACTICE (WORK SMART)

Leaders who believe in Working Smart have no fear of the dark. To these leaders, the VUCA world presents not a daunting, murky environment, but an unexplored treasure trove of mystery.

In the face of uncertainty, like the Work Hard leader, we could attempt to push out a path in every direction or fight through walls of confusion with head-on brute strength. But that is exhausting and unlikely to see us take more than a few steps forward.

Instead, we must be like the explorers of old and set sail in an agile ship, winding our way around the globe, dodging sea monsters, storms and pirates with the help of a trustworthy crew and a reliable sextant. Michael Tobin summed it up perfectly when he told us: "There is no such thing as work-life balance anymore. You've got to integrate them. Otherwise, you will fail miserably at one of them."

NEW AND CREATIVE APPROACHES

Leaders who use moments of adversity to find new and creative ways to achieve goals are more successful, more often. Tamara Rojo told us this: "As a principal dancer I learned what not to do, how not to lead artists, how not to suppress artistic freedom, how not to put dancers in boxes of the past. I learned to be more self-sufficient and more resilient.

Everything was a fight, but I would be able to put all the negative things behind me in order to put on a beautiful show. The ballet helped me cope."

As such, Work Smart leaders demonstrate a consistent array of behaviours. They are invariably:

- Expressive
- Optimistic
- Decisive
- Restless
- Empowering.

Leaders who strongly relate to this Journey Motivator think outside the box. If they are successful leaders, they are also natural optimists, refusing to waste energy on the things that have gone wrong. Instead of obsessing over missed forecasts, they simply move on.

Remaining positive and confident in their own, and their team's, ability to solve the problems confronting them is key to resilience. Here are six tips to help you do exactly that.[31]

1. **Time Yourself.** Author and time-management coach Jamie Novak[32] points out that few people actually assign a time limit to a task. "Sure, to-do lists make us more productive; so does grouping the tasks into batches and prioritizing them," she said. But that does not mean you'll get them done in the time you allotted, or that whatever you are batching won't end up taking over your day. The more you time yourself and become aware of how long a particular type of task takes you, the more time you'll be able to actually identify and re-purpose in your schedule.

2. **Use GPS.** No, not a global positioning system, but rather 'Goal, Purpose, Scope'. Mitzi Weinman,[33] founder of the TimeFinder coaching service and author of *It's About Time! Transforming Chaos into Calm, A to Z*, describes this version of GPS as similar to your car's onboard system in that it "gets us from one place to another." But when delegating, her GPS approach "helps you and the person to whom you are delegating stay on track." Weinman recommends beginning by determining objectives and setting goals and asking: "What does the work look like when completed?" The next step is understanding the purpose, the *why*, so you can explain how the work fits into a bigger picture. "That's how you get buy-in to a project," she said. Finally, provide the person to whom you're delegating the task with a full, 360-degree view of it. This could include deadline, format, audience, budget, available resources and your leadership involvement.

3. **Adopt Time Theming.** Mike Vardy, a productivity coach and founder of the Productivityist[34] consultancy, says this technique "frees one's mind to focus on the tasks that are critical to making progress in all areas of life." Time theming – assigning an overarching theme to a given afternoon, or perhaps a full day of the week – is a great way to avoid decision fatigue. Mike explained: "Theming your months, weeks and days gives you less to think about when you're trying to decide what to do because that time has already been given some sort of thematic value." This can also help ensure work-life balance.

For instance, every Friday could be themed 'friends day' and every Saturday could be themed 'family day'. By theming different priorities into your calendar, you can gain more freedom and flexibility to finally start creating a work-life balance that fulfils them.

4. **Create A New Email Strategy.** Email, which favours hard work over smart work, is a particularly insidious productivity killer. When tethered to email, people become engrossed in multitasking without even realizing it. For instance, you get notification of a new note, reflexively stop what you were doing and click on it. You then read through the item, decide to either respond or revisit it later, and perhaps get distracted by something else entirely at that point. You eventually circle back to your original task, where you have to take a moment to remember where you left off. This can leave a person feeling like they're constantly busy, because they're perpetually breaking concentration, shifting tasks and impacting their productivity. Vardy suggests that the 3Mail Workflow email strategy[35] can help free up your inbox. Start by creating a folder for every day of the week. During periods in your day designated for checking emails, either delete new items or place them in the appropriate day-of-the-week folder for future consideration. The goal is to never have any notes lingering in your inbox, having delegated them all to a specific day of the week.

5. **Don't Start from Scratch.** "Don't continue to re-invent the wheel; starting from scratch each time is a big time-waster," said Novak. Instead, she recommends finding and modifying templates you've utilized in the past. Or, try finding someone who's already done what you need to do and take a cue from them on how to proceed. This allows you to leverage other people or other resources in order to reach your goal as efficiently and effectively as possible.

6. **Leave Yourself A Note.** Interruptions or time constraints can't always be avoided. Whenever you need to stop a task before its completion, Novak recommends, "Leave yourself a note." This little reminder should detail where you stopped, she said, so you "can jump back in without wasting time backtracking to remind yourself where you left off and what you'd planned your next step to be."

Keep in mind that working smart comes down to finding the most efficient and effective way to reach goals. This often includes leveraging other people or resources and utilizing self-awareness to build on strengths and delegate when appropriate. The more self-awareness you gain about your work style, the more you can find ways to work smarter, not harder. Perhaps it is time that the expression 'work-life balance' is laid to rest and, in its place, we use the term iconic Michael Tobin uses, 'work-life integration'. In our 'always on' world, leaders who make this transition may well find that their resilience is strengthened because the mindset is about accepting and incorporating multiple demands upon our time and talents, not constantly attempting to keep a number of plates spinning at one time.

STEERING DEVELOPMENTAL EFFORT

One last thing to consider: leaders who work smarter, rather than harder, recognize where to invest developmental effort. This is important because there are different kinds of strengths and limitations – those capabilities formed over time by various combinations of nature and nurture, inheritance and experience.

Strengths acquired in areas consistent with personality and other inherited, stable characteristics may be thought of as 'natural strengths'. They feel comfortable and easy in execution. Conscientious people, for example, frequently find it easy to plan and organize since it appeals to, and is consistent with, their preference for order and discipline.

These strengths can easily be deployed and worked with, and developmental effort expended here might transform performance way beyond competence – propelling it into the realm of excellence – if the individual has the potential to do so.

Strengths acquired in areas that are inconsistent with one's personality always feel more fragile. Non-conscientious people can learn the skills and techniques of planning and organization, but they may never feel like second nature. Moreover, their performance in those areas may be inconsistent. Developmental effort in these areas will likely be required to prevent deterioration, much as the maintenance of a new language learned in adulthood needs constant practice. This may not lead to excellence, but to a level of competence that has to be worked at continually to be sustained.

Of course, there are also limitations that can be turned into strengths without a whole lot of effort. Such potential strengths are limitations until they are developed, but the presence of helpful attributes means that the skills required are easily learned and progress is often rapid. Developmental effort in these areas is high-yield and likely to be easy, well rewarded and enjoyable.

However, there are also limitations that are resistant to development. These are capabilities where there has been little learning to date and that are inconsistent with personality and other inherited characteristics. Developmental effort in these areas tends to be frustrating, progress tends to be inconsistent and acquisition of skill is slow. Rather than work on developing capability in these areas, it may be more helpful to consider a work-around solution. This would indeed be 'working smart'.

It is hard to be equally capable across the board. Typically, leaders develop unevenly, developing great capability in some areas and not in others. So, the best leaders are not necessarily well-rounded, although the best teams are. Strengths and limitations are modified by the way they are consistent or inconsistent with other attributes and capabilities.

This creates two different types of strengths and limitations. There are strengths that are natural and others that less well developed. There are limitations that are readily remediable and those that are much harder to change, or even resistant to change. Yet, in those areas where a leader has resistant limitations, it is possible to work with others whose capabilities are different but complementary.

A FLUID DYNAMIC

This is 21st century leadership: teams of competent, dedicated professionals working effectively together and moving the leadership focus as circumstances require. It's a dynamic that allows different leaders to take the lead as their capabilities become required and then stepping back into a more supportive role when others need to lead.

This is the power of the collective. For many organizations today, it is also an integral part of the need for diversity, especially diversity of thought.

"The fact that people are different should be recognized on a basic level, and leaders should proactively seek out people who fill gaps and challenge them in ways they hadn't thought of," John Amaechi told us. "With diversity we are metaphorically placing an item on the table and asking people to sit over on the other side and tell us what we can't see."

MY RESILIENCE REVIEW

Below are some questions relating to the Destination Belief of Resilience. Find a quiet place, contemplate the questions and write down your responses. Better still, verbalize them out loud. Doing so will move you along on the journey of applying The Leader's Secret Code.

Q1. Do you tend to take on all of the work yourself, or do you share the load?

Q2. How do you react emotionally to periods of challenge and adversity? What might this say about you?

Q3. How do you feel about your colleagues possessing skills or knowledge you don't have?

Q4. Are you comfortable with delegating responsibility? If so, why?

Q5. How are you inculcating mindsets and behaviours that encourage your people to show innovative thinking, manage their wellbeing and support others in times of need?

WHAT'S IN THE MIND?

The psychologist says ...

Leading in the VUCA world is a white-knuckle roller-coaster ride, and that's not likely to change any time soon. Whatever your balance of Journey Motivators, the ability to bounce back when you face adversity is likely to be your biggest asset.

In an article for *Dialogue Review*, Dr Liz Mellon, organizational psychology consultant and former executive director of Duke CE, described the key to endurance with this equation:

$$\text{Endurance} = \frac{(\text{Resilience} + \text{Adaptability} + \text{Perseverance})}{\text{Reserves}^{[36]}}$$

Mellon's endurance equation underlines many of the concepts we have explored above, such as the importance of an emphasis on Journey Motivator 2. Adaptability, she writes, is key when constantly changing circumstances mean leaders are unlikely to bounce back in precisely the same shape. Behaviours stemming from Journey Motivator 2 mean leaders will work just as well – or better – in their *new form*.

We also need perseverance. This gives us the energy to keep going until we achieve our goals. Meanwhile, underpinning the entire equation are your 'reserves'.

Think of yourself (or a leader you admire) as a champion marathon runner. These athletes are well-trained, experienced, ultra-conditioned winners. Their speciality? Like a leader's, it's playing the gruelling 'long game'.

When it comes to the mind and body, rest is just as important as work. The best athletes in the world understand the value of resting to recover before a match or event and their schedules are carefully planned to balance training and competition with rest time. Without proper rest, a top performer's accumulated fatigue greatly impairs their ability – and, Mellon notes, if we're running on empty, the entire equation could crumble at the first hurdle.

DEVELOPING RESILIENCE IN OUR PEOPLE IN CHANGING TIMES

As a leader, you also have the responsibility of promoting and protecting the energy and resilience of your teams. It is unrealistic for leaders and their team members to consistently operate with high energy levels; what is most important is the ability to recover high energy levels when required. In turn, this helps to embed a healthier human dynamic within the workplace. The biggest contributor to the need for resilience is change; how you as a leader and your team members respond to change can have an impact on performance.

Below is the Performance and Change Matrix. You can see that the concept is a simple one – a 2x2 matrix. Like many previous quadrant-based concepts that came before, this one may be simple in design, but it gives us a lot of insight and potential guidance as to how we as leaders respond at any given time, depending upon where we perceive the current position of each of our people to be on the matrix.

THE LEADER'S SECRET CODE

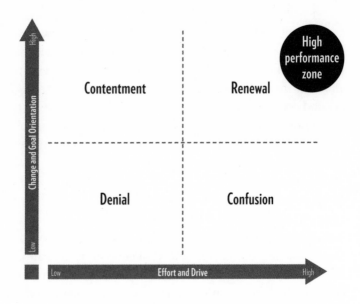

Let's just make sure that everyone is clear as to what the matrix is telling us. The vertical axis is the level of Change/Goal Orientation and the horizontal axis is the level of Effort/Drive required to achieve success in any given goal or objective. This means that in the bottom-left quadrant, low change/goal orientation and low effort/drive means that the individual is probably in denial about the change going on, or the work required to perform at the required level. Well, there is a leadership challenge for us! How do we take someone in denial and lead them toward renewal?

In the top-left quadrant we have someone who displays a high change and goal orientation, but who is making little effort despite this. Here we see someone who is in the contentment zone. They believe that things are just right. They see the need for change. They buy into the objectives, but the application is missing. So, how do we lead people who are content? How do we help them see that high performance will only come from a greater application of effort and drive? The we come to the bottom-right quadrant, where there is a low change/goal orientation, but lots of 'stuff' going on. What this means is that this type of person is lacking true focus. They know they want to be doing things and are trying hard, but their lack of focus and true alignment to the changes around them means that they are simply confused. If we stay confused for too long, we get chaos. So again, the challenge for us as leaders is to identify when we might have people who are in confusion and guide them toward renewal.

This brings us to the top-right quadrant, the renewal zone. Here we have people who have a high change/goal orientation combined with a high level of effort and drive. It's not all plain sailing for leaders of course, so ask this question: what might happen if someone is constantly in a state of renewal? The answer is that they might burn out – the renewal zone is a great place to be, but the role of the leader is to ensure that once our people are there, we balance the demands of being in the renewal zone with the appropriate downtime and chance to recharge. The beauty of this model is that you can use it through the lens of considering your people overall; or you could look at specific tasks and objectives you have set your people and ask which quadrant they are in relative to that task or objective. Understanding the matrix gives us choices in terms of our leadership and management approach and how we can navigate the Performance and Change Matrix for the best chance of success for ourselves and our team members.

THE LAST WORD ON RESILIENCE

Josep 'Pep' Guardiola is widely regarded as one of the greatest football managers of all time.

The iconic manager of Manchester City, the English Premier League football club, Guardiola earned that distinction not only based on the number of trophies he has accumulated working with the best teams in the world, but also for his legendary resilience. Few others have attained his heights and remained at the top for so long in so many different countries.

Guardiola's secret to resilience is his capacity to put himself and his own needs first. He believes foremost in his own philosophy and approach to life and sport. Harnessing powerful self-knowledge, he's able to maintain balance and stay recharged for longer periods of time than others in similarly stressful managerial roles.

That self-knowledge means that Guardiola, unlike other great managers, knows when to step away from the game. This is the critical factor in maintaining his resilience and performance at the highest level of leadership.

In 2012, Guardiola famously resigned as manager of FC Barcelona, the Spanish football giant. He'd won three successive Spanish league titles and two Champions League titles in the previous four years. When asked why he was choosing that moment to resign, at the height of success, Guardiola insisted he needed a complete break from being a leader and a chance to recharge his batteries.

No matter how low or great the moment, this leader recognized that he had been exhausted by his own intense approach to leadership and winning. He needed to find "peace," he said.[37]

Guardiola relocated 6,000 kilometres away, to New York City. He learned both English and German in the space of 12 months. Since his year-long sabbatical, Guardiola's record has been one of remarkable achievement. On his return to football he jetted off to Germany, took the helm at FC Bayern Munich and led the club to three German titles in three consecutive years. And then he went on to conquer English football with his new club, Manchester City.

Reflecting on the latter triumph, the manager-cum-philosopher noted that the move from European football to that of England required massive adaptation, resilience and learning how to work smart.

CHAPTER
FIVE

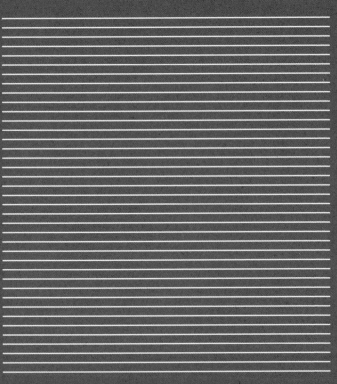

INFLUENCE

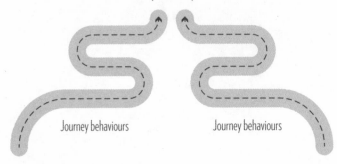

Destination Belief
Leadership is about how I make things happen through others
(Influence)

Journey behaviours   Journey behaviours

Journey Motivator 1
The degree of importance you attach to influencing using your authority and adherence to well-defined organizational structures and processes

Journey Motivator 2
The extent to which you believe in leading through encouragement and support and inspiring others to 'go above and beyond'

Transactional   Transformational

10 **10**

"It's amazing," coaching company CEO Michelle Braden wrote in *Forbes*, "how many people believe that once they obtain a certain title or level of leadership, people will automatically respect and listen to them. They believe that with that title comes influence."[38]

Tim Berners-Lee, the man who invented the internet, said: "The ability to influence others to buy in to your idea is often even more important than the idea itself."[39]

But, as Braden points out, leadership and influence are not interchangeable. It's true that titles and position may imbue you with responsibility, power and the ability to control the working lives of vast numbers of people. Results, however, come from something far more useful: the ability to have an impact on the character, development or behaviour of someone or something.

We spoke to the senior leaders in a number of our client organizations as part of our research for this book, yet we also quickly identified influencers who were often completely different individuals. One CEO we spoke to, who joined his company as an outsider, said one of his first critical tasks was to identify the influencers within his business – those, he said, who "did not reside on the leadership team."

Not too dissimilar from its angry cousin, manipulation, influence is extremely powerful and is a responsibility that should not be taken lightly. Like all Destination Beliefs in The Leader's Secret Code, it can be approached in two ways: as *transactional* or *transformational* influence.

Transactional Leadership, otherwise known as management leadership, was first proposed by the sociologist and political economist Max Weber[40] and explored further by organizational behaviour scholar Bernard Bass. It's an approach that emphasizes actual, physical transactions between a leader and his or her subordinates. The style focuses on improving the current situation of the organization by framing the steps taken to conduct business and controlling organizational activities.

THE LEADER'S SECRET CODE

TOEING THE LINE

Iconic chef John Campbell uses Transactional Leadership a lot. "I'm in control of everything that goes on within the business," he told us. Transactional leaders like John wield their authority to tiptoe the line between influence, coercion and imposition of their wishes onto those around them.

Whether they do this by carrot or stick, they are formidable individuals. *Forbes* describes them as being "focused on performance, driving hard and getting the job done."[41]

However, the benefits derived from this approach do not come without a trade-off. Typically, when the Transactional Leadership dynamic is in play, there is little personal bond between leader and subordinate. (Note that we deliberately use the word subordinate, rather than 'colleague' or 'team member' here!)

In contrast to that approach, the second Influence Journey Motivator centres on a leader's belief in leading by encouragement and support. Rooted in emotion, empathy and empowerment, Transformational Leadership is frequently found in organizations with more fluid or nascent structures, such as start-ups. Indeed, examples of Transformational Leadership can come from great adversity as opposed to great opportunity.

Pacifique Niyonsenga is a 27-year-old Rwandan artist and the founder of an artists' collective. A former street child survivor of the genocide, Pacifique is simply a remarkable person. Through his passionate commitment to improving the lives of street children, he is the embodiment of Transformational Leadership.

Pacifique lived on the street from the age of six and was fortunate enough to meet a Canadian missionary family when he was 12. They befriended him and helped him get an education. As an adolescent he saw that not every child living in poverty in Kigali was given such opportunities, so he decided to use his skills in drumming, dance and painting to unite friends in support of all those vulnerable boys and girls. At the age of 19 he chose not to join his adoptive family in moving back to Canada. Instead, he elected to stay in Rwanda and committed his life to helping others.

EMBRACING EVERY CHALLENGE

Pacifique embraced every challenge thrown at him, and together with talented artist friends he established the Niyo Arts Gallery in Kigali. Forty percent of the proceeds from each painting sold reverts to the gallery, which now cares for some 125 underprivileged children. They and their families pay no tuition and are given books, two meals a day and an annual social security allotment. In addition, Pacifique teaches them history and cultural skills. The children put on dance performances and create their own paintings, generating money that helps pay for their education, medical expenses and day-to-day needs.

Pacifique's dream is to buy the building that houses the centre, which is currently rented, and to build an improved shelter for impoverished children. One day he'd also like to construct a brand new Niyo Arts Gallery.

When we visited Pacifique and the children at the gallery it was evident from their dishevelled look that poverty is a very real challenge for them, each and every day. However, we also quickly noticed the sheer joy on their faces as they prepared to meet our strange party of guests. Every move, tune and beat of the drums radiated excitement, hope and joy. We learned they'd been preparing all day for the performance, since visitors like us help attract additional guests, recognition and support.

To say we were humbled by the experience is an understatement. Indeed, it's not an exaggeration to say that it changed us. We danced, drummed (badly) and laughed as we were led around the gallery, exploring the talented work of these young artists. A friend and colleague of ours now has two wonderful pieces from this inspirational little corner of Kigali hanging on the walls of his home in Boston, Massachusetts.

Pacifique has endured so many challenges, many beyond our wildest contemplation. Yet, he knew that he had to personally transform in order to fundamentally transform the lives of so many children. It's a monumental undertaking that he recommits himself to, day after day, year after year. Pacifique is an unexpected Transformational Leader who shines a light on how one person can overcome seemingly insurmountable odds by ensuring that his resourcefulness always outweighs his lack of resources.

As Pacifique so perfectly demonstrates, a leader who embraces this style brings about transformation (change) in those he or she is leading. Transformational Leaders work with their teams to define the desired change in the organization and then use their influencing power and enthusiasm to motivate their followers to bring about that change. They frame the requirement for a change in the existing culture, paint a vision, spell out the mission and implement the change, with the dedication and support of their teams.

In Transformational Leadership, the leader acts as a role model and a motivator who offers vision, excitement, encouragement, morale and satisfaction to the followers. The leader inspires his people to step up their abilities and capabilities, builds their self-confidence and promotes innovation across the whole organization.

The historian and political scientist James MacGregor Burns[42] first proposed this concept in 1978. The main idea of this leadership style, he suggested, is that both the superior and subordinate work to lift each other up, improving morale and motivation all around.

An effective modern leader, as John Amaechi explained to us, clearly "recognizes that he or she is constantly under scrutiny, and everything they do matters."

JOURNEY MOTIVATOR 1
MY INFLUENCE STEMS FROM USING MY AUTHORITY AND ADHERENCE TO WELL-DEFINED ORGANIZATIONAL STRUCTURES AND PROCESSES (TRANSACTIONAL LEADERSHIP)

"My rules, my orders – follow them."

Sound familiar? These are the words of a 100% Transactional Leader. They're the battle cry of one whose approach to leadership involves heavy influencing and (ab)using their authority and position to make others do what they want them to do. Such individuals are often preceded by their reputation.

Frequently observed behaviours in the Transactional Leader including being:

- Aggressive/dominant
- Opinionated
- Strong willed
- Confident/arrogant.

However, before bashing this style of leadership too strongly, we must consider the fact that many iconic leaders demonstrate a vast array of transactional tendencies. Tamara Rojo, for example, told us: "Because I see the bigger picture of the (ballet) company, I can sometimes lose empathy for the people. I need to remember that the people who will make this happen need my empathy. If some people can't make the journey, you have to stop the boat for them so people can keep up or walk out."

Tamara is indicative of our high-performing group. High-performing leaders demonstrate a remarkably balanced score of transactional and transformational leadership. Among top performers it is perhaps no surprise to find equilibrium because a transactional style succeeds in a crisis, as well as in projects that require linear and specific processes. Given that these two factors map to large parts of the VUCA world, we can begin to understand why this leadership style is relevant in today's business world. Many high-level members of the military, CEOs of large international companies and world-class sports coaches are known to be transactional leaders. Transactional leadership also works well in law enforcement and first-responder organizations.

Consider the following three examples:

PACKER-BACKER

"The price of success is hard work, dedication to the job at hand, and the determination that whether we win or lose, we have applied the best of ourselves to the task at hand."

– Vince Lombardi

Born in Brooklyn, New York, in 1913, Vince Lombardi is lauded as one of the greatest American football coaches of all time.

He signed a five-year coaching contract with the Green Bay Packers in 1959 and led the team to a 98-30-4 record, with five championships. His Packers won Super Bowls I and II, and the Super Bowl trophy is in fact named after him. He used to run the team through the same plays in practice, over and over. Their opponents knew the plays Lombardi would run, but the Packers were so well trained that many teams still had trouble defending against them. The coach became a symbol of single-minded determination to win.

FROM THE PROJECTS TO THE ESPRESSO BAR

"Starbucks is not an advertiser. People think we are a great marketing company, but in fact we spend very little money on marketing and more money on training our people than advertising."

— Howard Schultz

Howard Schultz was born in 1953 and grew up in Brooklyn's housing projects. He escaped "being poor," as he put it, through a football scholarship to Northern Michigan University. He worked for Xerox for a while after college and then took a job selling coffeemakers. One of his customers was a fledgling Seattle outfit called Starbucks Coffee, Tea and Spice Company, which originally sold bags of coffee beans (not made-to-order drinks). Schultz landed a marketing job with the six-location roastery in 1982 and two years later opened the first Starbucks coffeehouse, based on the concept of an Italian espresso bar. It was a success, and he was anxious to expand, but the owners wanted to stay small. Schultz left and opened his own Italian-style coffeehouse in 1984. With the help of investors he bought Starbucks in 1987 and merged the two companies. By 2006, Schultz was ranked 394th on *Forbes'* list of the 400 richest people in America.

SHOW AND TELL

"I believe if you show people the problems and show them the solutions, they will be moved to act."

— Bill Gates

Like a horse chomping at the bit, determined to win the race, from an early age Bill Gates sat transfixed at his computer screen, clenching a pen between his teeth, immoveable until the job was skilfully completed. Gates' ability to focus deeply, shutting out all distraction, has enabled him to influence a vast range of people and situations and drove decades of growth for his IT behemoth, Microsoft. The world's richest man is an implementer, a doer and an iconic transactional influencer. He has also been called anti-competitive, dictatorial and a controlling overseer, consistently hands-on and ever-present at HQ. Gates' influence – and that of leaders who similarly relate to the Transactional Journey Motivator – manifests as 'show and tell', inspiring teacher-student behaviours. *I explain, you listen and we take it to the next step.* As a Transactional Leader, he used to visit product development teams and ask difficult questions until he was satisfied that they understood the goal and were on track to meet it.

As one might expect in considering one of the most influential people of our age, there have been claims that Gates has a reputation for being blunt, even combative. It is generally acknowledged that Gates was a popular leader among those most like him, although others found his style very difficult to deal with. In his autobiography, Paul Allen, Gates' erstwhile friend and Microsoft co-founder, observed this effect.[43] Whatever opinion one might have of Gates' style, his success is surely proof that there is a time and a place for Transactional Leadership.

We must recognize that the Influence Destination Belief delivers less significant leadership impact than any other. We know this because high and low performers score similarly. Therefore, there is not enough delta to conclude that high performers are excellent leaders because of their use of influence alone.

So, what's going on?

ONE OR THE OTHER – OR BOTH

We've found that while most definitions of leadership include the word 'influence', the statistical relationship between both variables may not exist as strongly, or as widely, as assumed.[44] According to Steve Graves: "You can influence without being a leader, and you can lead without influencing."[45] Indeed, many of the leaders we spoke with understood that they've found themselves needing to influence scores of people over whom they had no direct authority.[46]

Here are some connections – and some distinctions – between leadership and influence:

- Leadership is visible, while influence may not be
- Leadership is usually conscious, but influence may be unconscious
- Leadership is seen every day – in every act within the organization – while influence goes on continually but might not be overtly evident
- Leadership inspires the company culture; influence propels the company culture
- Leadership is seen by all, while influence runs beneath the surface – it is 'the water cooler conversation'.

So, since we know that high and low performers score similarly on Journey Motivator 1, can we expect to see similar alignment on Journey Motivator 2? Let's find out.

JOURNEY MOTIVATOR 2
I LEAD THROUGH ENCOURAGEMENT AND SUPPORT AND INSPIRING OTHERS TO 'GO ABOVE AND BEYOND' (TRANSFORMATIONAL LEADERSHIP)

Influencing through inclusion requires time – time for each individual member of the team, time for listening and time for discussion.

Patience, charm and charisma are on abundant display among such influencers. They believe in a reciprocal relationship based on a win-win outcome, to the benefit of leader and team member alike. They go to great lengths to foster a customized approach, showing respect for every member of the team. They invest time and energy in people, to ensure that they feel cared for and have a voice, while leaving everyone clear and comfortable with their task and how to complete it.

Strong bonds are formed between leaders with this Journey Motivator and their teams. Trust and loyalty can blossom easily. These leaders serve others, for as Michael Tobin told us: "I work with people based on trust, not on skill sets or anything else. I'll gladly employ someone that can't do a job as long as I think I can trust the guy. They can learn a job; you can't teach him trust."

John Campbell agreed: "The fundamental core of all leaders is trust, and you have to trust that person 100%. You have to trust that the leader will eat last, that the leader will take money last, that the leader will take praise last."

EMBRACING COMPROMISE, DIVERSITY OF THOUGHT

This Journey Motivator is not transactional, but transformational. Transformation requires compromise and embracing diversity of thought, especially on the part of the leader.

Unsurprisingly, descriptions of Transformational Leaders include behaviours and characteristics like:

- Facilitator
- Sociable
- Empathetic
- Compromising/indecisive
- Persuasive.

Using the 20-point allocation system as explained in Chapter 1, the research showed that when it comes to Influence, top-performing leaders are prepared to adopt transactional and transformational influence in equal measure. A *blended leadership* perspective emerges, combining transactional and transformational leadership behaviours. This is consistent with other research showing that employees whose leaders exhibit transformational leadership not only perform well, but are also satisfied with their company's performance appraisal system.

Additionally, organizational behaviour expert Bernard Bass asserted that "the best leaders are both transformational and transactional."[46] He also explained how "transformational leadership adds to the effect of transactional leadership" and a combined approach leads to "the extra effort and performance of followers."

AN AMALGAM OF BEHAVIOURS

This all suggests that leaders who exhibit a melding of transformational and transactional behaviours are much more effective; as such, the top-performing leader becomes an authentic brand.

These individuals can deliver clear instructions and communicate the path that needs to be followed – step-by-step, in a professional and personal manner – while being present as a guide to support the team throughout the voyage. In essence, the leader is congruent in what they say and what they do, something we've seen as incredibly important to organizations wanting to win the war for talent. As John Amaechi mentioned to us: "Millennials have a razor-sharp sensitivity to incongruence."

For those who relate more strongly to the first Journey Motivator, the key to growth is to listen more. Balancing out one's perspective with other viewpoints and opinions and getting the team to come forward with analysis and observations will ensure that the best decisions are made. These leaders need to arrive at the summit of their pioneering journey *with others* and not alone; otherwise, what's the point? This is something that leaders with an affinity for the second Journey Motivator understand perfectly.

Social media can help. Year after year, the power of social media grows exponentially. World leaders use it daily to directly reach the person on the street, ensuring that their undiluted message reaches the widest possible audience as quickly as possible.

According to the Pew Research Center[48] in Washington, digitally native Millennials are now the largest generation in the US labour force and outside of work they represent $200 billion in annual buying power. Simply put, smart business leaders must get comfortable on social media if they want to engage in successful internal communications with their employees and successful external communications with their customers.

True social leaders like Richard Branson and Elon Musk, the latter of Tesla and SpaceX fame, understand the importance of social media and have millions of followers to show for it. Yet there are other senior business executives who outsource this critical task to entry-level marketers – or unwisely skip it altogether.

THE DOUBTER, THE BROADCASTER, THE SUPERIOR

In his 2014 book, *A World Gone Social: How Companies Must Adapt to Survive*,[49] Mark Babbitt, founder of the young professionals' social community YouTern, highlighted three types of leaders who've yet to take the social media plunge. He dubbed them the doubter, the broadcaster and the superior.

Perhaps you can identify yourself as one of these. This is how they're characterized:

- The **doubter** still doesn't believe that social media is here to stay. Instead, this person sees it as a fad and a waste of both the leader's and the organization's time. While other industry competitors use social strategies to build communities and create brand ambassadors, the doubter's company misses out.

- The **broadcaster** hasn't fully grasped the power of social. While this leader is comfortable using social networks, he or she participates in one-way communication – an old-school 'push' strategy of pumping out content but failing to engage with and listen to the company's followers.

- The **superior** is ruled by ego. This leader feels invincible and believes that the rules of social media don't apply to him or her. Leaders like this mistakenly think that their executive status can protect against public backlash if they say something controversial or insensitive, but they're quickly corrected when such incidents occur.

When leaders avoid social media, the impact doesn't just fall on the companies they run. By failing to engage with the public at large – even those who aren't direct customers – business leaders miss the opportunity to become established thought leaders and build personal brands outside of their businesses.

"You, as an individual and a leader, can go places that your company's brand cannot,"[50] said Ryan Holmes of Hootsuite Holmes.[51] "*The New York Times* is not going to accept a contributed article from Virgin, but if Richard Branson wanted to write an article, they'd take it. And that's because it's him, not the company. People want to hear from people." At the end of the day, people buy people.[52]

MY INFLUENCE REVIEW

Below are five ideas relating to the Destination Belief of influence. Find a quiet place, contemplate the ideas and write down your reflections. Doing so will move you along on the journey of applying The Leader's Secret Code.

1. *Know the people you want to influence*
   We are most influenced by people who know, understand and respect us. Having influence over someone won't come overnight. Spend time getting to know your team and showing them that they can trust you and work with you. In his book, *The 7 Habits of Highly Effective People*, educator and author Steven Covey[53] says: "Seek first to understand, then to be understood."

2. *Aim to be liked and respected by those you seek to influence*
   People want to be led by people they like. This does not mean you are their 'best buddy', but it does mean you're seen as a concerned, engaged leader who's connected to both the vision of the team and to the people individually. Reflect on your relationship with the people you want to influence and determine what may need to change.

3. *Commit to the people you want to influence*

   If you are not committed to your team, why should they have any reason to listen to you? People are influenced by people they can rely on. Your team will be motivated to listen to you when they can tell you're invested in them. Otherwise, there will be a lack of trust and a lack of change. Find ways to show your team that you're committed to them on a group and on an individual level.[54]

4. *Engender mutual commitment to help influence thrive*

   Commitment works both ways. In order for influence to occur, you need to be committed to your team, but they also need to be committed to you. When they are committed to you and your vision, you will easily be able to gain their influence. Have conversations with your team to discover what they're truly committed to and help make sure everyone is on the same page.

5. *Be strong, focused and a good example to those you want to influence*

   When you set a good example, people will naturally want to follow you. Position yourself as a leader with a strong goal and the ability to meet that goal. People want to follow people who are going somewhere.

WHAT'S IN THE MIND?

The psychologist says ...

Your effectiveness at influencing others will impact how people judge you, your chances of promotion, whether or not your ideas hold power, your ability to engage colleagues and the quality of your business relationships. Persuasion and influence are mission critical skills not only in your professional role, but all aspects of your life. We will all know someone who is influential to us; someone who can shape our view, move us to a destination or motivate us to move outside of our comfort zone. Many well known world leaders are known for their influencing skills: Martin Luther King Jr, Bill Gates, Emmeline Pankhurst and some may even add Donald Trump to this list. Why? Because Trump has been influential, albeit using a technique that some will have liked and some will have hated.

In the Transactional Journey Motivator, influence is described as "the degree of importance you attach to influencing your authority and adherence to well-defined organizational structures and processes." We introduce the push/pull influencing style to establish how this may portray itself back in the work environment to you as a leader. The push/pull model explores the ways in which leaders exert influence to reach organizational goals. Influence is exerted through a mixture of two different styles. It is either forced (pushed), or encouraged (pulled). The Journey Motivator of Transactional aligns to that of the push influencing style, specifically the Directive quadrant of the model below. The Directive method is useful in times of urgency, where a deadline is looming or a safety issue exists and is a good technique to use with solid, well-defined ideas and direction. Push leaders will say "I want …" and are more 'I' or 'self-focused'. It is also good to use if you have inexperienced people in your team who require a little more direction than those with experience. However, if this style is overused, you may come across as arrogant, uncollaborative and a bit of a bully, so it is important to remember the optimal balance of this motivator.

The Transformational Journey Motivator maps nicely to the other part of the push/pull model, Pull and specifically the quadrant named 'Collaborative'. The clue is in the title of this method where the leader follows a more team-focused approach and seeks the involvement of others through discussion and idea-generation. Pull leaders will say: "We are…" and this method is particularly successful when you need commitment, you are looking for innovation and creativity and if you have no clear answer for the challenge you are looking to solve. If this style is overused, you may be perceived as weak or lacking authority.

The other two related styles are Persuasive, another push method which is best used when there is a specific issue that needs addressing and the leader wants to present a logical, objective and even-handed argument. This style is most successful when your personal knowledge is high and you have credibility with your audience, when you know you have the 'best' answer, backed up by research and you need buy-in to a decision that is going to be unpopular. Be warned, when over-used however, you may be seen as manipulative and self-serving. Finally, the other Pull method is Visionary; used when there is a need to connect with the emotions of others and to enable them to visualise how things might be. This is most successful in circumstances where you are at the start of a change process. New ideas will be required and you need to challenge mindsets and entrenched beliefs. You want innovation and creativity to come from others. If over-used, you may be seen as a constant 'dreamer', over-idealistic and lacking common sense.

PUSH	PULL
Directive	Collaborative
Persuasive	Visionary

As with all the Destination Beliefs, it is important to remember that there is no 'one' style to adopt. As a leader, it is important you take into consideration the situation, the people involved, the outcome you are trying to achieve and adopt the most suited style. That is not to say you are then wedded to this way; experiment with moving around the four quadrants to experience each style and reflect back on whether you achieved your desired outcome.

THE LAST WORD ON INFLUENCE

THE DAY THE NEW WORLD CAME OF AGE

If you ever visit the beautiful Vineyard Hotel near New-bury, UK, you will not fail to notice a large mural called the 'Judgement of Paris'. It depicts a moment in time when the accepted order of things changed forever: the great and the good of the wine world gathered together for a tasting which might today seem perfectly normal, but which back in 1976 represented revolution.

It all started when Steven Spurrier, an English wine merchant with a shop in Paris called Les Caves de la Madeleine, was urged by his American business partner to hold a blind tasting event. While Steven was in love with everything French, his partner Patricia Gallagher wanted to raise awareness of US wine.

Steven organized nine of the most prestigious French wine experts to act as judges. They included Aubert de Vil-laine, the owner and 'Grand Monsieur' of the Domaine de la Romanée-Conti, the most famous winery in France, and Christian Vannequé, head sommelier at La Tour d'Argent, one of the most famous restaurants in Paris. Their task was to compare French and Californian wines.

Spurrier selected the best of the best French wines, and he fully expected them to be superior – he never had any intention of importing and selling California wine in Paris. All of the French wines were from vineyards that had been trading for centuries, often in the same family hands,

194

whereas the Napa Valley wineries had been started in the 1960s and were run by hippies with little or no previous experience.

The result of the blind tasting was that California wines won both the red and white categories. In fact, in the white category, three of the top four winners were from California. No one could have predicted this outcome. The experts hadn't even expected the California Chardonnays and Cabernet Sauvignons to come close, let alone win. The general reaction could best be described as shock and awe. The 2008 movie version of the story, starring Alan Rickman, is in fact called *Bottle Shock*.

This simple event had a significant influence on the worldwide wine market and the French standing within it. It influenced how retailers and consumers make decisions about wine, and we see that France is now competing head-to-head with the US, Australia, Argentina, Chile, South Africa and perhaps even the UK.

It all goes to show that you can change the mindset of others, you can disrupt traditional markets and thinking, and you can have a global economic impact ... all through the most basic of approaches.

CHAPTER SIX

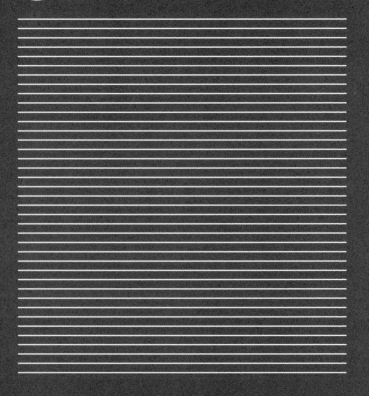

COMMUNICATION

Destination Belief
A good leader knows how to communicate with their people and wider audiences, inside and outside their organization (Communication)

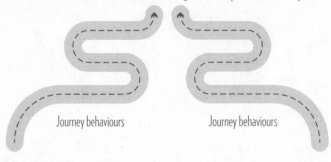

Journey behaviours   Journey behaviours

Journey Motivator 1	Journey Motivator 2
The extent to which you believe the use of fact-based and rational tones will best deliver your communication message (logos and ethos)	The degree to which you believe in the importance of permitting personal vulnerability and emotional appeal (pathos) to permeate your communications

Unemotional   Emotional

  8 12

Communication is not unique to humans. From the hive mind of the bee and the cells of a sponge, to the mating calls of birds or the plethora of dolphin dialects, communication is the way every species on Earth transfers information from one party to another.

At a time when communication (and miscommunication) has never been easier, effective communication is a vital skill.

In his seminal work, *On Rhetoric*, Aristotle[55] produced one of the first examinations of communication and the art of persuasive speaking and writing. In his study of communication techniques used by actors, merchants and politicians, Aristotle identified three elements of persuasive communication: *ethos*, *logos* and *pathos*.

Ethos, the Greek word for 'character', is a method of convincing an audience of your credibility, authority and the veracity of your proposition. We can generate *ethos* by choosing language appropriate for the audience, employing correct grammar and exuding rhetoric. *Ethos* is essential for leaders – especially those with less experience – as it can be used to build an impression of your authority, competence and credibility. It's especially useful as a more resilient substitute for confidence; this relies on circumstance and self-belief, whereas *ethos* can flow directly from a leader's capability.

Logos comes from the Greek for 'reason'. It comes into play when one persuades with logical thought and facts, employing data, charts, percentages, case studies and expert testimony to make your reasoning irrefutable. Used correctly, *logos* cements a logical conviction in your audience. As a decision-maker, is a conversation really complete without capturing the stakeholders' minds through *logos*?

Pathos, from the Greek word for 'feeling', is used to evoke a stirring emotional connection with what you're discussing. Consider the last great speech you heard. Did you feel anything? Were you moved to a particular action or reaction? The best speeches, pitches and conversations build *pathos* by using 'light and shade'. This involves fast and loud words to convey the excitement of moving forward to achieve one's hopes and dreams (light), interspersed with slow whispers or dramatic pauses to drive home why maintaining the status quo is unattractive (shade). *Pathos* prompts the listener to relate to the beliefs, ideals or strategy you're proposing. It is your human connection, your call to arms, your request for volunteers. Here is where great leaders are made.

Our research revealed that all leaders believe in the power of effective communication. Whether they're effective communicators is of course another matter entirely.

As with the other six elements of the Secret Code, there exist two Journey Motivators for Communication. Journey Motivator 1 derives from the first two of Aristotle's elements, *logos* and *ethos*. Conversely, Journey Motivator 2 encapsulates Aristotle's third element: the emotional, human *pathos*.

Using the 20-point allocation system explained in Chapter 1, the research showed that when it comes to Communication, top-performing leaders awarded 12 points to emotional communication and 8 to unemotional.

JOURNEY MOTIVATOR 1
FACT-BASED AND RATIONAL TONES
(LOGOS AND ETHOS) WILL BEST DELIVER
MY MESSAGE (UNEMOTIONAL)

There are a million pieces that work together to propel you forward as a leader, but ultimately, it's about how you connect with others.

Regardless of whether you're setting a vision, being creative or pushing for results, your success will boil down to how well you communicate. And the more people you lead, the more critical your communication is.

Iconic leader Bruce Daisley told us: "I don't sugar-coat my communications. I am quite direct." Michael Tobin presents a similar perspective, saying: "I'd put myself as an *eight out of ten* on being impatient, but my demeanour says otherwise." And you'll recall John Amaechi saying earlier that he quit shouting 30 years ago, after realizing that whenever he raised his voice, he'd "lose people for a week".

Harvard Business School Professor Boris Groysberg writes in his book, *Talk Inc*,[56] that the "higher you go in an organization, the more you must engage other people in conversations, rather than trying to shout them into submission." This view is consistent with our research, which found a significant difference between communication styles at different hierarchical levels. The executive level, for example, demonstrated several precision-focused styles, as outlined below.

The rational, unemotional style senior executives often exude can be described as:

- Analytical
- Data-driven
- Detail-oriented
- Impatient

As we've said, analytical thinking is logical, data-driven and rational. It's the objective, factual part of the brain that immediately asks: 'Why?' As one successful leader told us: "In God we trust. All others must bring data."

As part of your communication, you need to be sure you're speaking to the analytical section of your audience. In order to best convey your message, you must show your analytical side, by showcasing the facts and proof that will earn you trust and credibility.

LEVERAGING YOUR LEARNING EXPERIENCES

A number of leaders we spoke with made reference to their own learning experiences.

One leader of a Fortune 500 company spoke of an immersive leadership experience he'd participated in a few months earlier, as part of a Duke CE leadership event. In that exercise, a team of real barristers used the adversarial setup of the courtroom to air arguments for and against a series of company-specific issues that were high on the executive leadership agenda.

"I remember seeing the (role-playing) legal team in their wigs and gowns," he told us, "and the sudden sense of importance descended on us all." He and the other participants spent time researching, structuring and delivering a series of cogent, persuasive arguments, aligned with whether they were prosecuting or defending the relevant issues.

What became evident to all was the need to always back up each and every argument with clear and compelling evidence – the facts. Many leaders who participated in the 'At Court' event said they came to understand that for years they'd been approaching things the wrong way. They realized that they'd tended to ramble on with lots of facts and data points in the vain hope of landing on a clear point, as opposed to starting with a clear point and then backing it up.

You only have to watch a single series of the TV show *The Apprentice* (either the US or UK version) and listen to the participants on the losing team beg, plead and seek to convince that they shouldn't be fired. Without too much analysis you will notice that the participant who understands clarity, structure and ordering (propositions backed up by facts in support) usually lives to see another week of challenges. For instance, they might say: "Lord Sugar, you should not fire me as I am the strongest participant in front of you (the proposition). I have been in three out of five winning teams. This is my first time in the boardroom bottom three. I have won two awards for my work, built a successful start-up at the age of 25, and during the task this week I sold three items, completed one negotiation and finalized the successful sales figures (the facts)."

Geil Browning, founding CEO of the organizational development firm Emergenetics International,[57] found that 67% of the population has at least a preference for analytical thinking, albeit usually mixed with other types of thinking. If analytical thinking drives an employee, they're typically sceptical and have a sound, deductive thought and reasoning process.

A TWO-WAY STREET

As a leader, communication must be a two-way street – intake is just as important as output. Strong analytical thinkers will latch onto information intake, so ensure that you give them the right kind of data. Analytical employees will also respond well to questions that ask them to prove a point and show evidence, so don't be afraid to be upfront and ask for it. This will help you gain respect and build trust.

There are various ways you can speak and interact more analytically, to draw out your analytical employees and position yourself as one who desires and values a rational, fact-driven approach:

1. **Encourage open-endedness**
   Push for investigation and examine all areas of a problem.

2. **Ask for research**
   Make sure your people are getting what they need, to in turn give you the data you need.

3. **Highlight important information**
   You need to show the big picture, not just the details.

4. **Provide a case study**
   Analyse past successes as a way of helping your team develop new ideas.

5. **Provide an overview as well as objectives**
   Clarity about your needs is critical.

6. **Use analytical phrases**
   - What is the cost/benefit of this project?
   - I need more information; this doesn't make sense to me
   - Let's get to the point
   - Let's explore this in more depth
   - What's the bottom line?
   - What does the research say?
   - There are many layers to consider
   - I value your investigation of the facts
   - I've been analysing the situation
   - Can we quantify this?

And with that, you have tools to help you think and communicate like an analytical leader.

Remember, whether analytical thinking is your preference or not, you invariably have people on staff whose brains work analytically. You need to have them engaged and believing that you understand them and the way they think.

JOURNEY MOTIVATOR 2
PERSONAL VULNERABILITY AND EMOTIONAL APPEAL *(PATHOS)* SHOULD PERMEATE MY COMMUNICATIONS (EMOTIONAL)

Without *pathos* it can be difficult for people to listen to your message.

Michael Tobin says: "I'm not a great fan of data and facts and figures. I think you can you can use data to justify whatever you want to justify. And I think the standard human approach is to come up with a thesis and then run around finding things that will prove it."

In a culture dominated by brand and image, *logos* – and particularly *pathos* – are all that is required to gain influence. An effective communicator knows that as long as the content is refined, polished and packaged well (*logos*), the audience will be moved toward an intended direction. Furthermore, a skilled communicator knows that if listeners are on the edge of their seats, hanging on every word and locked in the emotion of the moment (*pathos*), the room will build toward applause and maybe even a standing ovation.

As the audience, we want what we want, when we want it: and we often want it now. We want our ears to be tickled with words that we can easily follow, we want to be entranced by them and we want to feel positive emotions in the process. As long as it leads to bliss, we're okay with ignorance. We will listen, watch and go wherever we're led. We have become sheep in our consumption of rhetoric.

Leaders who use *pathos* effectively demonstrate a number of specific characteristics. They're seen as being:

- Empathetic
- Authentic
- Easily distracted
- Emotive
- Passionate.

There is a potential problem here, which is that *logos* and *pathos* are dependent upon *ethos* for the long-term positive or negative impact they have. *Logos* and *pathos* can be immediate in their influential power, delivering an impulsive peak of fickle fame. When *ethos* is added to the mix it becomes interesting. If *ethos* confirms the *logos* and *pathos*, the influence soars and has the potential to become timeless. However, if the *ethos* contradicts the *logos* and *pathos*, the influence crumbles ... and often very quickly. In that moment, the *logos* and *pathos* become an indictment of the messenger and while the content and connection may remain 'true', they are exposed as a manipulative veneer.

FORGOTTEN, OVERLOOKED, AVOIDED

Ethos is the most important anchor for a leader, but because it's not required for initial influence it's often forgotten, overlooked or simply avoided.

Communicators today are being lulled into believing that their polished words and powerful points of emotional connection are the secret sauce of success, leading to long-term influence. Reality whispers a loud contrast. *Logos* and *pathos* are pathways to immediate influence, but unless *ethos* is deepened, matured and safeguarded at all costs, their influence will not be effective.

Accordingly, the highest-performing group of leaders score this Journey Motivator at a higher level than the unemotional communication style. The distribution of points, using the method explained in Chapter 1, was 12-8 in favour of the emotional (*pathos*) approach.

Brain surgeon Peter Lees is a high-performing leader who demonstrates this optimal balance. "In healthcare," he told us, "we seem to believe that we interact with patients with one skill set, and with colleagues, with another. Hence, many doctors are expert in the highly challenging art of imparting bad news to patients, and yet hopeless in doing the same with colleagues over, say, performance issues. Most doctors would not knowingly talk about colleagues in front of them, and yet they will talk about the most intimate details regarding patients by the bedside."

"Leadership development is now much more commonplace for clinicians and communication skills feature highly," Peter said. "Do we bring our complex communication skills, learned from many years of interacting with patients and families, to other work interactions? I think not. As our colleagues are the same species as our patients, is this logical? I urge you to think of your 'clinical interaction' skills and how these can be tweaked and used to good effect in your managerial or leadership roles. And I think you'll be pleasantly surprised by how much you already know."

Karen Penney sees the link between leadership communication and how effective people can be. She says, "Jobs are not jobs for life these days. We move on and leaders change often. The more people are in the dark, the more they worry and concentrate less on their role and being effective. They put two and two togther and make sixty-three. They begin to create new 'truths' which, if not dealt with, can rapidly become perceived wisdom, even though they are far removed from reality. You know the kind of thing: 'We saw this and that must mean that…and it's doom and gloom.' It might sound extreme, but it's not. If you don't communicate they will come up with a narrative which fills the vacuum. Now, it may be that you have to communicate that you have nothing to communicate! I make a point of almost over-communicating. I may have to say to people that I don't know what changes are coming but, when I can share, I will. I make every effort to ensure that people feel that I am being open and not hiding things. This will free people up to focus on the things they should be doing. Communication is a combination of giving people the facts and connecting with the emotions of people. It is also about ensuring that people see the link between what I am being asked to do and where the company is heading. Take someone who looks after 20 clients. My role as a leader is to help them see that that when they help those clients it is contributing directly toward the strategy set by the CEO. I make sure that they think, 'If I help these people today and every day this is how I link to the direction of the business.' At the top of the business we all talk in high level terms, but people need to know how they fit in. It is very important to have a link from the strategy of the business to your sense of purpose. You feel valued. You can see where you fit and you can talk about it with authority and pride. I want my people to be able to say, 'This is the contribution I make.' My leadership role is to translate high level strategy into something meaningful."

MY COMMUNICATION REVIEW

Below are some questions relating to the Destination Belief of Communication. Find a quiet place, contemplate the questions and write down your responses. Better still, verbalize them out loud. Doing so will move you along on the journey of applying The Leader's Secret Code.

Q1. What factors potentially limit my ability to truly listen to my people? In what ways will I be different going forward?

Q2. Do your people hear from you like a sudden lightning strike (incisive strike and that's it), or like rolling thunder (more of a constant rumbling presence)? What do you want to keep the same, or change? (Think about this in the context of the balance of logos, ethos and pathos).

Q3. Are you curious enough about your team? If not, what will you do differently to demonstrate an interest in them?

Q4. What are you doing to support efficient and meaningful communication within your team?

Q5. Which members of your team do not communicate as well as they could? Can you do something productive about that?

WHAT'S IN THE MIND?

The psychologist says ...

Many people have a tendency to suppress, ignore or dismiss feelings, especially when they are uncomfortable. Over time, this habit reduces one's capacity for self-awareness, limiting our potential to perform. Businesses that lack EQ may see rigid or defensive behaviour in their people, poor team working, low levels of personal resilience and reoccurring emotional outbursts. Businesses high in EQ benefit from more engaged employees and leaders, staff who are more able to adapt and cope with change, better team working, collaboration and innovation.

Science has shown that feeling precedes thought and behaviour. The business evidence is clear; taking emotion out of work does not increase employee engagement, drive customer satisfaction or build high performance – managing emotion effectively does. One of the most important aspects to good communication is EQ. This is how somebody manages their personality to be both personally and interpersonally effective, but how can this affect our communication?

There are many different EQ models available in the marketplace and many have a common theme which focus on Daniel Goleman's five main aspects:[58]

1. Knowing your emotions
2. Managing your emotions
3. Motivating yourself
4. Recognising and understanding other people's emotions
5. Managing relationships.

First and foremost, let's explore knowing your emotions. How often are you fully aware of what you are feeling? If you are unsure how you feel about something, it can be very difficult to communicate. Have you ever tried explaining how you feel about something when you just don't know? It can be very difficult and while it may seem obvious to know what you are feeling from moment to moment, sometimes we simply do not. How we are feeling can impact our body language as well as how we verbally communicate. We can all relate to getting home from work after having a bad day and your spouse hasn't started dinner as agreed; you might communicate differently about this if you had had a good day instead of a bad one. If you have an ability to recognise and accept that you are tired and a bit irritable after a bad day, your awareness of these emotions allows you to manage them. The third aspect of EQ, motivating yourself, goes without saying in a leadership role; you may wish to look forward at the 'The psychologist says' pages within Chapter 9, of Fulfilment, to read about intrinsic and extrinsic motivation.

The last two domains of EQ focus on others and on being able to recognise and manage relationships. Based on our example above, you get home and the dinner isn't started, but you identify immediately through body language and facial expressions that your spouse is extremely upset by something. Being able to recognise this emotion will affect how you respond to the fact the dinner has not been started. If you didn't recognise this emotion and raised your voice, it would probably result in an argument and both parties being more upset than before. EQ allows us to work better with people, understand them and communicate with them. It gives us choices in how we choose to communicate with others in any given situation, resulting in a higher probability of success of your desired outcome.

THE LAST WORD ON COMMUNICATION

WHEN LISTENING SAVE LIVES

Much is written about communication, as indeed we're doing here. However, as part of that conversation, the last word has to go to that undervalued skill of listening.

For this story, we return to a cold night in the early hours of the morning in London. This time the location is Archway Bridge, originally designed by the architect John Nash and created in its current form in 1897. Today this historic pedestrian bridge traverses the busy A1 highway, which links north of London with the city centre. Over the years, however, it has become known by another name: suicide bridge.

It's around 2am and police have received a report that a male in his 30s has climbed over the bridge's barriers and is threatening to jump to the road, some 80 feet below. Uniformed officers arrive and, in an unfortunately well-rehearsed routine, close the busy highway in both directions and try to initiate a conversation with the obviously distressed young man.

Nearby, in a sleepy suburban street, a phone rings and Kevin O'Leary, the on-duty hostage and crisis negotiator, is immediately *on the job*. He has a full day's work behind him and this extra duty is disturbing another night's sleep, but someone has to do it.

As Kevin arrives on the scene, uniformed colleagues gladly step back to let him take 'point.' It's quickly determined that the man has been drinking and is distressed over a domestic incident with his estranged wife that's put contact with his children in question.

At this point many of us would feel the need to rush into action, talk too much (and too excitedly) and try to convince the man to step away from the edge. Not Kevin. He is the epitome of calm, steady, poised and quiet. Only a few open questions from Kevin and then ... silence. Space to listen, to understand, to reflect and to decide on next steps.

Kevin often jokes that his wife says he must "bore them down" from the edge, which he admits isn't too far from the truth. "It's not about rushing to solve the problem, but patience in allowing the person to vent," he told us. Police officers are trained and conditioned from their first days on the job to become take-charge problem solvers, but those skills are the antithesis of what's needed in a crisis negotiation.

FROM VENTING TO VISION

Giving someone in this situation time to express their frustrations allows for the gentle transition from venting to vision – what their world might look like if they could choose. After some time, Kevin recognized the moment when he could probe a little and this led to the question: "When do you think you'll be able to see your children again?" The young man's reply was the turning point: "I suppose she'll let me when I stop drinking."

It was a telling response – his vision of a future when he would see his children and recognition that there was something he could do to help make that happen. It would be a tough journey for someone grappling with alcohol addiction and anger-management problems, but one that he was apparently willing to pursue.

The conversation changed direction completely. They were now exploring possibilities, and there was optimism, in a 180-degree pivot from hopeless act that had been contemplated that night.

There were no magic solutions, no superhuman capabilities, that changed the fortunes of a father that night. Kevin says this was one of those nights when his training as a negotiator was proved to have been right. Listening – truly listening to someone – lets you share their perspective and understand their view of the world. And from there, new possibilities emerge.

CHAPTER SEVEN

STRATEGY

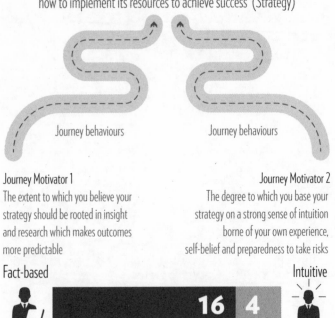

Destination Belief
Strategy is about knowing where an organization has to position itself and how to implement its resources to achieve success (Strategy)

Journey behaviours

Journey behaviours

Journey Motivator 1
The extent to which you believe your strategy should be rooted in insight and research which makes outcomes more predictable

Journey Motivator 2
The degree to which you base your strategy on a strong sense of intuition borne of your own experience, self-belief and preparedness to take risks

Fact-based

Intuitive

16   4

Described perhaps best as 'indulging in a risky delusion',[59] trusting your instincts can quickly lead you down the wrong road.

Don't worry, nine times out of ten it probably isn't your fault. You see, your brain and 'instinct' evolved at a time when one was stressed by things like a mountain lion heading toward you, your club left behind in the dust. Instinct is based on something called *heuristics*, which is a neuroscientist's way of saying 'shortcuts' or 'rules of thumb.' It's a simple proposition: you see a lion, you run. The fact that the lion may not be hungry, or might not give chase, does not occur to your primordial *fight or flight* instinct.

But the boardroom doesn't have lions, so why should you think twice before building strategies? The VUCA world does not play by the rules of the old, established corporate landscape. Where once you would have to traverse a country to inspect stores, or dine with suppliers to keep them sweet, today you can automate the former and cycle through suppliers for every product you market. Where once market research had to be conducted by hand, over months, social media platforms will manage it in seconds. In a VUCA world, there's nothing to say that a lion is even a meat eater.

Your heuristics – your instincts – are no longer so sure of what to do.

Let's say you're interviewing a new applicant for a job and you feel something is off. You can't quite put your finger on it, but you're a bit uncomfortable with this person. They say all the right things, their resumé is great and by all indications they'd be a perfect hire for this job. Except your gut tells you otherwise.

There's a persistent, gnawing uneasiness and you know that choosing the wrong person could have terrible consequences. Should you go with your gut?

WELL-PLACED SUSPICIONS

In such situations, your default reaction should be to be suspicious of your gut. Research shows that job interviews are actually poor indicators of an employee's future performance. Unfortunately, research also suggests that most employers[60] tend to trust their guts over their heads and give jobs to people they like and perceive as part of their 'group', rather than the most qualified applicant.

In other situations, it actually does make sense to rely on gut instinct to make a decision.[61,62] Consider Colin Powell's '40-70 Rule'. Powell, the former commander of US Armed Forces and Secretary of State under President George W. Bush, was a strategist, diplomat and leader. He asserted that we need 40%-70% of the total available information to make a decision.[63] Working with anything less than 40%, Powell said, we're bound to make the wrong decision. However, if you wait for more than 70% of the information, too much time will have elapsed and others will have made the decision (for better or worse) and moved on. It will then simply be too late.

Research suggests that we as humans can tap into our intuition to fill the 30% gap.[64] We all want to be right and we all want the available information, but the reality is that things change too quickly and too frequently for this to be a reality for any leader. While the 40-70 rule may not be for everyone, the need for a blend of intuition and information is almost certainly our reality for some time to come.[65]

A 2013 Duke CE study, *CEOs' Perspectives on the Changing Leadership Context*, identified two primary issues as leaders grapple with this conundrum. First, challenges are less predictable these days, and second, knowledge is less reliable. Many CEOs felt that it was now impossible to predict future changes and that with increased global interconnection, current mental models are no longer accurate as change accelerates.

Duke's research presented seven 'sense abilities' that may help leaders to survive and thrive in times of constant change:

1. Develop an ability to *sensemake*, to enable you to quickly see how to leverage for action. The challenge is to understand the context you are in and your own position within it. The pressing question will be: "How long can I hold onto multiple conflicting hypotheses about which course of action to take until I can see a way forward that gives me the greatest leverage?"

2. Lead through successive approximation. Leaders must cultivate the ability to make forward progress, even though complete information is absent. A key question you must contemplate for this 'sense ability' is: "How can I quickly figure out the next move that will leave me with the most options for subsequent moves?"

3. Build and influence collectives. We've all heard the phrase, "What got us here may not get us there". For many leaders, the muscles they used to drive decisions and actions are not as effective now as they may have been in the past. There is now a need for a deep appreciation of context and the ability to form

collectives of individuals and entities that can take on questions – and solve problems – together. The key question here is, "How do I engage people in a way that builds understanding and movement? Essentially, how do I inspire and bring people with me?"

4. Develop reliable sources of knowledge and insight. The continuing speed of change in the world and the number and kinds of information outlets make any leader's role more challenging. Therefore, leaders must cultivate and curate a more diverse personal network and broader set of trusted knowledge resources to 'widen the lens'. These resources need to go beyond their company and business. The critical question is: "How good is my radar for picking up weak signals that could undermine my business, or for identifying new opportunities to grow?"

5. Engage the organization in the new rational. It is not only the leaders who can lose their footing. Turbulence over the years has defined rational behaviour in many organizations as *avoidance of risk* and *following the rules*. What followed was loss of confidence, decision paralysis and the inability to take advantage of opportunity. It is the leader's messages and actions that can redefine the rational behaviours of the organization. A central question becomes: "How do I move the default position of the organization from avoidance of risk to the pursuit of opportunity when the context seems less certain?"

6. Understand how to understand. Leaders are dealing with new and complex issues in unfamiliar contexts. One CEO told us: "Senior leaders have to be able to look at the bigger picture, and that picture has no frame." This goes to the relative importance of better understanding *the unfamiliar* over trying to absorb what might be known today in a technical sense. The most valuable knowledge may not be 'what is' but '*why* it is'. The question becomes: "How can I make sense of unfamiliar contexts as quickly as possible?"

7. Broaden systemic self-awareness. Understanding the leader's impact on systems and situations that go well beyond the walls of the company is central to building his or her ability to navigate unfamiliar contexts. The key question here is: "What could be the systemic consequences should I choose to take a particular course of action?"

Yet research on decision-making shows that most business leaders don't know when to rely on their gut and when not to.[66] While most studies have focused on executives and managers, research shows the same problem applies to doctors,[67] therapists[68] and other professionals. One should also consider the subtle yet important differences that take place when one moves from individual to team decision-making and then on to a corporate decision-making process.

FIGHT OR FLIGHT

So-called gut reactions are rooted in the more primitive, emotional and intuitive part of our brains that helped ensure survival in our ancestral environment. Tribal loyalty and immediate recognition of predator, friend or foe were especially useful for surviving and thriving in that environment.[69]

In modern society, however, our actual physical survival is much less at risk. Generally speaking, our gut is more likely to compel us to focus on the *wrong* information as we make decisions in the workplace, at the store, when investing and on the home front.

For example, is the job candidate mentioned above – the one you have a vague, gnawing uneasiness about – similar to you in race, gender and socioeconomic background? Even seemingly minor things like clothing choices, speaking style and gesturing can make a big difference in determining how you evaluate another person. Research on nonverbal communication[70] reveals that we like people who mimic our tone, body movements and word choices. Our guts automatically identify them as belonging to our tribe and being friendly to us, raising their status in our eyes.

This automatic emotional reaction represents the 'autopilot' system of thinking,[71] one of the two systems of thinking[72] in our brains. It makes good decisions most of the time, but also regularly makes certain systematic thinking errors that scholars refer to as cognitive biases.[73]

The other thinking system, known as the 'intentional' system, is deliberate and reflective. It takes effort to turn it on, but it can catch and override the thinking errors committed by our autopilots. This way, we can address the systematic mistakes made by our brains in our workplace relationships and other areas of life.

A POINT OF DEBATE

Keep in mind that the autopilot and intentional systems are only simplifications of more complex processes and that there's debate in the scientific community about how they work.[74] However, for everyday life, this systems-level approach can be useful in helping us manage our thoughts, feelings and behaviours.

In terms of tribal loyalty, our brains tend to fall for the thinking error known as the 'halo effect', which causes some characteristics we like and identify with to cast a positive halo on the rest of the person. Its opposite is the 'horns effect', in which one or two negative traits change how we view the whole.[75] Psychologists call this 'anchoring', meaning we judge this person through the anchor of our initial impressions.

Now, let's go back to our job interview example. If the person went to the same university you attended, you're more likely to hit it off. Yet just because a person is similar to you does not mean she'll do a good job. Likewise, just because someone is skilled at conveying friendliness does not mean she'll do well at tasks that require technical rather than people skills.

The research is clear that our intuitions don't always serve us well in making the best decisions – and, for a business person, bringing in the most profit.[76] Scholars call intuition a troublesome decision tool that requires adjustments in order to function properly.[77] Reliance on intuition is especially harmful to workplace diversity and paves the path to bias in hiring, including in terms of race,[78] disability,[79] gender and sexual preference.[80]

This problem was highlighted for us in clear terms by John Amaechi when he told us: "The need for interpersonal comfort will trump organizational change, every time." That's a clear warning about the cookie-cutter approach to recruitment, antithetical as it is to embracing diversity of thought. "It's a leader's role to accept others who are different." The physical form he said, is "just the package that carries a person's brilliance. Do you want the brilliance, or do you want the convenience of having someone who makes you feel more comfortable in this current moment?"

GUT REACTION VS ANALYTICAL DECISION-MAKING

Despite the numerous studies showing that structured interventions are needed to overcome bias in hiring,[81] business leaders and HR personnel tend to over-rely on unstructured interviews and other intuitive decision-making practices.[82] Due to the autopilot system's overconfidence bias[83] – a tendency to evaluate our decision-making abilities as better than they actually are – leaders often go with their guts on hiring and other business decisions, rather than using analytical decision-making tools that have demonstrably better outcomes.

A good fix is to use your intentional system to override your tribal sensibilities.[84] In this way you'll make a more rational, less biased choice that's more likely to result in the best hire. You could note ways in which the applicant is different from you – and give them 'positive points' for those differences. Or you could craft carefully structured interviews[85] with a set of standardized questions, which are asked in the same order with every applicant.

So if your goal is to make the best decisions, avoid such emotional reasoning, which is after all a mental process in which you conclude that what you feel is true, regardless of the actual reality.[86]

Validation of instinct is your new secret weapon in strategic thinking. As Jonas Salk, who discovered the polio vaccine, noted: "If we combine our intuition and our reason, we can respond in an evolutionary sound way to our problems."[87]

According to our research, top-performing leaders expertly combine inner wisdom with a knowledge of systematic and scientific data to make well-rounded strategic decisions – which, ten times out of ten, are the best decisions. Karen Penney puts it like this: "You have to be wary of not slowing things down because you use data to justify your actions. I would always say listen to your gut; but in order to sell an idea you will need to have the data in the background. In my current role I am about to launch a new partnership. It could be transformational. I always knew it in my bones, but the data is informing our actions – where to launch and how to launch etc. Your gut and the data are very important, but the more you go up the food chain the more you will need to have the data. You need that gut feel because the data could lead you in a whole range of directions. It's only your experience, your personal knowledge, that allows you to select the pathway that you believe represents the right way. Frankly, that is where your passion will show through. Data does not have passion. We leaders spread the passion and energise and invigorate others to use the data in the right way."

JOURNEY MOTIVATOR 1
ANALYZING DATA AND RESEARCH WILL ACHIEVE MY DESIRED OUTCOMES (FACT-BASED)

"It is a capital mistake to theorize before one has data."[88]
– Sir Arthur Conan Doyle, author of *Sherlock Holmes*

Leaders who have an affinity with this Journey Motivator depend on facts. Historical facts; results that have happened. They thrive on proof of results and research from the marketplace that is both measurable and quantifiable. These are the bedrock for this Journey Motivator to formulate a winning strategy.

The Fact-Based Leader will usually be seen as someone who is:

- Detailed
- Analytical/insightful
- Impartial and disconnected from personal, softer matters and emotions.

Impersonal evaluation of information and data helps formulate a set of conclusions that helps drive implementation of the strategy. Leaders who strongly relate to this Journey Motivator value historical data to determine long-term goals and shorter-term action plans – strategy formulation as well as deciding on the allocation of resources.

At their best, these leaders discuss and present the 'what happened' and the 'whys', with particular interest in the 'therefores', drawing conclusions from research and insight into business strategy.

THE AVAILABILITY AND USE OF DATA

And that's why the key to this Journey Motivator's success is the availability and use of data – for these leaders, having the latest and most up-to-date information at hand is essential. Many algorithms determine the probability of outcomes using this Journey Motivator's insight, leveraging data and research on the external marketplace as well as the internal facts and results. The Journey Motivator trusts this information implicitly.

The highest-performing group of leaders were assessed as scoring 16 out of 20 points (as explained in Chapter 1) when it comes to adopting a fact-based strategy. Of course, there is a potential downside here. Without access to a full set of detailed analytical data and research, they're lost ... and found sorely wanting when making strategic decisions. They are focused on what has already happened and try to carry that success forward, while attempting to circumvent weaknesses in the strategic equation.

Bruce Daisley told us the following: "Everyone has an opinion around the table, but that's just not what we are here for. Unless you can causally prove something about a product, we will never change the strategy. Only if one thing causally drives another will it change."

It is for this reason that top leaders balance their strategic decision-making using an optimal balance. We already know that they lead with a Fact-based Journey Motivator, but this means that an Intuitive Journey Motivator is still a very important aspect of a top leader's strategic approach.

JOURNEY MOTIVATOR 2
TRUSTING HEAVILY IN WHAT MY EXPERIENCE AND MY GUT FEELING TELLS ME WILL LEAD ME TO THE CORRECT DECISIONS (INTUITIVE)

Recent insights and discoveries in the field of neuroscience have given new credibility to the role of intuition in leadership, especially when it comes to decision-making.

At their best, leaders who embrace this type of Journey Motivator rely on their intuition, their gut feeling and then look to back it up and confirm the decision with facts. They take action based on their own vision and have a strong sense about people. They can anticipate trends and move with great confidence through any situation they're faced with. And, consequently, they take action without waiting for facts and figures.

Terms that usually apply to these Intuitive Leaders are:
- Wise through experience
- Sees the 'big picture'
- Problem-solver
- Brave
- Risk-taker
- Empathetic.

Leaders who identify strongly with this type of Journey Motivator can reach into many facets and understandings they've gained through their career to finally settle on a decision. They will then be proactive when unforeseen circumstances arise, to stay on track to achieve the end goal.

They have an innate ability to know what needs to be done when they see early warning signs of deviation from their strategy and can manoeuvre and utilize resources and people effectively to achieve their goals, allowing nothing to slow their momentum.

Passionate as they are, they expect the rest of the team to embrace the same attitude.

They do not need a roadmap or factual information at the outset to come to a big-picture conclusion.

The potential danger with this type of Journey Motivator is that the destination may remain out of reach if, after the facts are presented, they aren't taken into account and the strategy isn't readjusted where necessary. However, such leaders are in tune with their environment and the wider world; they have their finger on the pulse. They are quick to see pitfalls and are able to prepare, only occasionally needing to realign the strategy to still reach the destination.

SO LITTLE KNOWLEDGE OF HUMANITY

One profession where this is particularly prevalent is the medical sector. We asked Peter Lees, who has worked for more than 30 years within the UK's NHS – the largest single-payer healthcare system in the world – what makes the service's staff tick. "It is astounding in a service established to care," he said, "that the running of it seems to display so little knowledge of humanity."

Peter has identified three lessons, which are universally applicable to using intuition within a fact-based environment:

Lesson one: "Shouting at 1.3 million people doesn't work."

Lesson two: "At the most challenging time in the history of the NHS, hundreds of additional actions are likely to be unwelcome, and it's hard to get people to do things they don't want to do." (Right. Anyone who's had children will understand this!)

Lesson three: "There is a very simple concept called discretionary effort. It's the difference between the amount you could put into your job minus the minimum to avoid being sacked."

Peter continued: "As we have stopped pay rises and perks don't exist, I conclude that the increased effort to get us out of the current abyss has to be free, based on goodwill. In other words, discretionary effort. Quiz time: will you get more discretionary effort by being nicer to people or by being horrible to them, making their lives more difficult, making it easier to prosecute them? If you struggle with this concept, Google the Harvard Business School paper *Putting the Service-Profit Chain to Work*."[89]

A VIRTUOUS CIRCLE

He cited evidence that if doctors and senior administrators are nicer to staff, the staff will be nicer to patients – a virtuous circle.

"Subordinates do not have a monopoly on fear, doubt, despair, uncertainty or anger. And while they are entitled to look to the leader for courage, certainty, optimism and calm, they are not entitled to trap a boss on an emotional pedestal," Peter said. "Learned helplessness is said to be all around us. I am often asked by younger colleagues what they can do without the trappings of high office. There are many answers, but one thing we all have control over is how we behave ourselves."

He went on: "Why do some of the people I trained with, who bemoaned the way we were treated, perpetuate the same poor behaviour of many of our forefathers?

One simple action for all of us is to reflect on our own behaviour – can we read the recent (General Medical Council) report on bullying with a totally clear conscience? When did we last say thank you to someone junior or someone senior? I could go on, but you get the point!"

And with that, he quoted his late mother: "Peter, if you can't say anything nice, shut up!"

John Amaechi also shared his thoughts with us on leaders repeating behaviours they had experienced in their early days. "Many leaders in our organizations are older and more experienced. Many of them were treated terribly and they therefore think they went through that phase, and as a result they are now a great leader. This is where the 'snowflake' (entitlement) label for millennials has come from in the workplace, with the view that the younger ones 'don't want to go through what I went through'. Some feel it was a rite of passage, and it's definitely not."

John repeated a term he used earlier in our conversation, saying that it's 'energy expensive' for leaders to create, evolve and sustain an environment that enables people to deliver optimally.

LESS COMFORTABLE THAN USUAL

Say you've known someone in your work for many years, collaborated with her on a wide variety of projects and have an established, professional relationship. You already have certain stable feelings about that person, so you have a good baseline.

Now, imagine yourself having a conversation with her about a potential collaboration. For some reason, you feel less comfortable than usual. It's not you – you're in a good mood, well-rested, feeling fine. You're not sure why you're not feeling positive about the interaction, since there's nothing obviously wrong. What's going on?

Most likely, your intuition is picking up subtle cues[90] about something being off. Perhaps that person is squinting and not looking you in the eye or smiling less than usual. Our guts are good at picking up on such signals, as they're fine-tuned to pick up signs of being excluded from the tribe. Maybe it's nothing. Maybe that person didn't get enough sleep the night before, or her allergies are acting up. On the other hand, she may be trying to pull the wool over your eyes. When people lie, they behave in ways that are similar to other indicators of discomfort, anxiety and rejection and it's hard to tell what's generating these signals.

All things considered, this is a good time to take your gut reaction into account and be more suspicious than usual. The gut is vital to our decision-making, to help us notice when something might be amiss. Yet in most situations where we face significant decisions about workplace relationships, we need to trust our head more than our gut in order to make the best decisions.

A surprising number of psychologists and academics view acting on intuition as a vital counterpoint to more deliberate choices based on intellect.[91] For example, intuitive consultant Sonia Choquette, author of the bestseller, *Trust Your Vibes at Work*, says: "When you follow your gut instincts you are putting something very natural to work. Your intuition will take you beyond the threshold to a place that reflects your most passionate interests and nature."[92]

When you hear that, smile. That's great news. Being called crazy[93] because your ideas make others uncomfortable is, in our experience, one of the surest predictors of success.

When you're acting based on research and reports, you're basing your choices on consensus – what everybody else is thinking – and innovation doesn't happen by committee.

When you act on your gut, you're unpredictable. Mercurial. Authentic. You make leaps of logic and see connections others miss. Gut instinct lets you see beyond where your business is today to what it could be tomorrow.

The famous Apple 'Think Different' commercial hit it right in the bullseye when it said: "Because the people who are crazy enough to think they can change the world, are the ones who do."[94]

THE UPSIDE OF 'NUTS' THINKING

Here are four examples of how counterintuitive, radical, 'you're nuts' thinking led courageous people to some profound successes:

- **Adam Werbach** was the president of the Sierra Club, an august environmental organization that dates from as early as 1892, when he decided to take a job consulting for Walmart, one of the largest corporations in the world. Werbach's idea was to bring about change from the inside, and he succeeded: in 2007 he helped Walmart introduce its Personal Sustainability Project (PSP), which has helped more than 40% of the company's employees embrace environmentally sustainable practices.[95]
- **Henry Ford** faced falling demand for his cars and high worker turnover, so in 1914 he did something that probably made other barons of industry go pale: he doubled his employees' wages. Crazy? Well, within a year, turnover dropped by a factor of more than 20 while productivity nearly doubled.

Demand for Ford cars boomed because the auto-maker's own workers could now afford the product they were making.[96]

- **Bill Allen** was CEO of Boeing in the 1950s, when the aeronautics company was making planes exclusively for the defence industry. But Allen had a crazy idea. He would build his own commercial jet that would serve what he was sure would soon be a booming industry: civilian air travel. So, he bet the future of Boeing and convinced his board to risk $16 million (in 1950s dollars) on a new transcontinental airliner, the 707. The move transformed Boeing and air travel.[97]

- **Travis Kalanick** faced serious headwinds when his rideshare service Uber instituted surge pricing. Charge customers more for your service when demand is highest or driving is more difficult? Seriously? The controversial CEO's move seemed sure to anger and alienate. Sure enough, there was heavy pushback. But Uber stuck to its guns, leveraged the law of supply and demand, and modified its surge policy when appropriate. Say what you want about Uber; dynamic pricing is now an accepted aspect of its business, and even companies like Disney are experimenting with the concept.[98]

Sometimes, decisions or ideas that seem insane – and are sure to infuriate everyone around you – are necessary to bring about change or move the world forward. Being able to make those calls based on the intuitive belief that they're right is one of the hallmarks of great, visionary leadership.

MY STRATEGY REVIEW

For this review we offer you a short story instead of questions.

The future of the kingdom

Once upon a time a King ordered his two sons to build two large aqueducts to supply water to his country estates, which were in a very poor state due to a great drought.

The first son took part of his father's riches and part of the army. With them he travelled north, where he ordered the people of those lands to work hard on building the aqueduct. He oversaw the work very carefully, paying the villagers fairly and finishing the project within the predicted two years.

Proud of his work, he returned to the palace, only to find the place in the midst of celebrations for the upcoming coronation of his brother as King. He was told that his brother had taken only one year to build his aqueduct in the south, and that he'd managed to do the job with hardly any soldiers or money.

This seemed so strange to the first brother that he began to investigate the southern aqueduct. What he found amounted to more than a few irregularities. He returned to the palace, telling his father to avoid this madness of making his brother King.

"Why do you say that?" asked the King. "Is there something I should know?" The Prince replied:

"You know how much I love my brother, but he must have gone crazy. He has dragged our good name through the gutter. He built his aqueduct deviating from the plans. He created so many outlets that barely half the water arrives at the royal estates. He confronted the Prime Minister in front of the villagers and he left without paying any of the workers. He even used your soldiers as labourers. And who knows, maybe that's only the start."

The King, gazing affectionately at his son, replied: "My son, what you say is true. Your brother had the initiative to modify the aqueduct to improve it; he had the wisdom to propose something which would improve the lives of everyone. He convinced the villagers to work quickly and without pay. He had the courage to confront the Prime Minister to defend justice and the charisma to set his soldiers to work even more hours than the villagers. His commitment was so great that he himself was the one who worked hardest on the project, forgetting his Princely status."

The King, seeing that the Prince was stunned and bewildered, delivered the moral of the story: "You know what, my son? This is why everyone adores your brother and would do anything he were to ask of them. He is more than their King ... he is their leader."

The Prince left, deep in thought. He came to recognize that the words of his father indeed pointed to the greatness of his brother. And without hesitation, he ran to his brother, to congratulate him.

WHAT'S IN THE MIND?

The psychologist says ...

Imagine a CEO of a FTSE 100 company announcing an important decision within the business because it feels right. This would be met with disbelief, a lack of support and concern in the ability of the CEO. Surely these decisions require logic, rationality and data to back up the decision? Indeed, relying solely on intuition may be a dangerous game and has a bad reputation; analytical thinking and access to large amounts of complex data has never been easier, so why bring emotion or intuition into the process?

Emotions are actually not silly responses that always need to be ignored or even corrected by rationality. Emotions are assessments of what you have just experienced or thought of − in this sense, they are also a form of information processing. Intuition or gut feeling is a chemical response in the body as a reaction to the information the individual has just processed and for that reason, they are important. Research suggests that the brain is a large predictive machine, constantly comparing incoming sensory information and current experiences against stored knowledge and memories of previous experiences, and predicting what will come next. This is described in what scientists call the "predictive processing framework". This ensures that you are able to deal with the different situations, challenges and experiences you deal with on a day-to-day basis as efficiently as possible. Your brain creates 'Cognitive Models' to help manage each situation you face and searches for help in decision-making as and when it is required. This matching between prior models (based on past experience) and current experience happens automatically and subconsciously. Intuitions occur when your brain has made a significant match or mismatch (between the cognitive model and current experience), but this has not yet reached your conscious awareness.

For example, you may be running on a footpath in the dark and listening to some music when suddenly you have an intuition to change to the other side of the road. As you continue, you notice how uneven the other side of the footpath was and you only just missed a raised path where the tree roots have broken through the tarmac. This would have tripped you up and potentially caused you injury. You are glad you relied on your gut feeling even if you don't know where it came from. In reality, the person in the far distance in front of you also crossed the road at this point (since they are locals and know the path well) and you picked up on this without consciously noticing it.

In the psychological literature, intuition is often explained as one of two general modes of thinking, along with analytic reasoning. Intuitive thinking is described as automatic, fast and subconscious. Analytic thinking, on the other hand, is slow, logical, conscious and deliberate. We can relate this to our two Journey Motivators of Intuitive and Fact-based. People often take the partition between analytic and intuitive thinking to mean that the two types of thinking styles are opposites and you are one or the other. However, a recent meta-analysis – an investigation where the impact of a group of studies is measured – has shown that analytic and intuitive thinking are typically not correlated and could happen at the same time.

Therefore, for every situation that involves a decision based on your assessment, subconsciously, you will need to be aware whether your intuition has kicked in, assessed the situation and come to a decision, or if you need to analysis and assess the situation before you. Is it a situation you have seen before, or is it completely new?

Perhaps it's time to stop over-thinking intuition and see it for what it is: a fast, automatic, subconscious process-ing style that can provide us with very useful information based on past experience that deliberate analysing and data collection can't. We need to accept that intuitive and ana-lytic thinking should occur together and be contemplated against each other in difficult decision-making situations.

THE LAST WORD ON STRATEGY

THE FÜHRER'S STRATEGIC ERROR

Adolf Hitler's habit as a meddler in military operations was legendary.

Frequently overriding the decisions of (and executing) his generals when they disagreed with him – 84 of them in total – it really was a case of 'the leader's strategy is *the* strategy'. Although he often ignored his generals' advice and the factual evidence that influenced their suggestions, one particularly disastrous intuitive decision stands out: the invasion of the Soviet Union in 1941.

Setting out in June, Operation Barbarossa saw the mighty German army march on the USSR and proceed to annihilate it. As Hitler had guessed, the Soviets stood little chance alone against him. With all going to plan, German troops paused on the outskirts of Moscow to recuperate and await orders from their Fuhrer.

"Take Moscow!" implored the Commander-in-Chief, Field Marshal Walther von Brauchitsch. "We can deal with the rest of the country later; let's cut the head off the snake."

However, the southern regions of the USSR – oozing oil, fertile fields and glory of victory – were too tempting to an arrogant Hitler. Drunk on his own intuition and success so far, the Führer fired von Brauchitsch on the spot, replacing him with a pliant nobody. "We will come back for the city later," Hitler announced.

Hundreds of miles away, the German army turned their backs on the walls of Moscow and headed for the rich countryside. Yet in doing so, stubborn, distrusting and overly reliant on his own instinct, Hitler committed possibly the grandest *faux pas* of them all: he forgot to check the weather forecast.

In his quest for glory, his troops, outfitted in light summer garb and with meagre rations left from their march across the plains, returned to Moscow to find a blanket of snow and a wall of ice. Winter had arrived. Kits disintegrated as frostbite chewed at the worn men. With no food from the land, weakened and freezing, 200,000 Germans were killed in a matter of weeks.

The disaster marked the beginning of a very different war and an outcome that, had that one naysayer been heard in Berlin mere weeks before, could have been completely different.

It's important to address the behaviour of leaders who cling too tightly to intuitive tendencies, megalomania and unilateral decision-making power. As author Ron Rosenbaum said: "We may despair of ever explaining Hitler. But we cannot abandon the attempt, because of those 'others' – the other Hitlers who may be among us even now."[99]

CHAPTER
EIGHT

EMPOWERMENT

Destination Belief
My people will feel empowered to take action and be the best they can be
(Empowerment)

Journey behaviours   Journey behaviours

Journey Motivator 1
The degree to which you believe that you should allow your people to assume accountability and ownership for success and what they learn when things go wrong

Journey Motivator 2
The extent to which you believe in the importance of providing your people with clear boundaries as to the limit/extent of decision-making and action

Ambiguous   Unambiguous

14   6

Employee empowerment is one of the most important and popular management concepts of our time. Distributing power and enabling others to meet their allocated responsibilities – and progress to new heights – prevents both you, the leader, and your corporation from becoming overwhelmed and slow.

There's an old adage: 'If you want something done right, you should do it yourself'. Go back and read Chapters 3 and 4 on Control and Resilience. If you think you can successfully run an entire company alone, and do so for a long time, you are invariably going to find yourself mistaken.

But, for those of you who still wish to try, consider the following question: can a single actor play both Romeo and Juliet in the same show? Usually not, though some actors have tried and succeeded. However, the fact that they usually can't is not a reflection on that actor's (possibly) extraordinary talent, unfailing memory or even boundless energy and passion. With scene after scene calling for the two characters to be on stage at once, trading lines and sharing at least five kisses, it is nearly physically impossible. It is not a failing of the actor, but just a metaphysical reality of the human condition.

Accepting this 'empowers' the casting of a second actor: a proven superstar or a new dynamo who will see the show make it to the end of its run. This is where a trusted network and open lines of communication become so important.

These two factors are not just important when empowering other leaders, either. Corporate leaders often find themselves in the role of actor, director, producer and head writer – and so much more – all at the same time. This can mean that some duties, such as rigging lights and serving up catering, need to be taken off the leader's hectic to-do list and credited to other members of the production team.

If that is going to work, however, we again require trust and communication and, within more rigid structures, a true culture of empowerment and incentives for employees to reward them for assuming responsibility.

In their book, *Empowerment Takes More Than a Minute*, the authors Ken Blanchard, John P. Carlos and Alan Randolph[100] illustrate three actions that organizations and managers can use to empower employees:

1. Share information with everyone
2. Create autonomy through boundaries
3. Replace the old hierarchy with self-directed work teams.

Iconic leader Michael Tobin told us: "I look for people who are looking to create leaders beneath them. Find the best person and create space for them, and drive that down to each level." This view is also mirrored by James Knight, who told us: "Guys in the Marines who were most impressive were the ones who were happy to be led by the most junior person. They recognized that teams are not simply hierarchical due to years served, but those with most value to add."

These views are endorsed by Professor David Pendleton of the UK's Henley Business School,[101] who calls on leaders to create what he describes as "complementary contributions". Rather than invest in the low-yield activity of trying to become skilled in those areas where we have *resistant limitations*, it may be better to surround ourselves with those whose skills are different from, but complementary to, our own. This means seeking out colleagues whose natural strengths are in those areas where we have resistant limitations.

Justin Ferrell of Stanford University's design school specializes in 'design thinking'[102] and regularly advocates the need for 'Radical Collaboration'. This is the idea that bringing together radical viewpoints and opinions will deliver breakthrough insights and in turn transformational change, as opposed to working only with people who are 'like us' and accomplishing marginal, iterative change.

John Campbell agrees. "If you go back some 2,000 years," he said, "the only reason we're still on this planet is because we collaborated with people and we were human to people, and that's the simplicity of an organization. That's how an organization in my belief should work, and that's just been my model forever. If you can connect to a human without an agenda, with trust and believability, you can do anything. It literally is as simple as that."

Such a notion is instantly appealing since it means we can always play to strengths: our own as well as those of others. This appeal is obvious, but so is the inherent difficulty of having to work with those who are least like us.

The advantages of this approach far outweigh the disadvantages, but it's also important to stress that this does not suggest excusing incompetence. It is not acceptable to argue that having a resistant limitation exonerates us. Tempting as it may be, you can't insist that your shortcomings in the area of planning and organizing are resistant limitations. It's *not* okay that you're chaotic and unreliable. A deadline is a deadline and a promise is a promise. Your colleagues need to be able to count on you no matter what.

So, what can you do? There are several actions that can, and must, be taken. To that end, consider playing through this internal conversation:

- I have to acknowledge the issue and not hide from it. Denial may be a tempting road to travel but I know that I'm not good at planning.
- I have to continue to recognize the importance of my shortcomings. I may encounter players who say it's okay for them to be somewhat chaotic because

they're so good at the things that really matter. The truth is that all the leadership tasks matter.

- I have to put the mitigation in place. My personal failings in planning and organization have to be addressed, usually by ensuring that there's someone on my team who is outstandingly good at it. And, I have to give them the clear mandate to lead me and the rest of the team in this aspect of our work ... and I need to be held accountable along with everyone else.
- I have to defer to them. There is no point in my overruling their decisions in this space: they know and I do not.
- Finally, I cannot absolve myself of responsibility in this area. I am responsible for my schedule, plans, organization and the like. My colleague may act on my behalf, but if things go wrong, it's still my responsibility and everyone needs to know that.

This approach takes us in the direction of greater diversity, but it's not the racial and gender diversity we generally think of, although it's compatible with those imperatives. It is instead a matter of seeking out, deploying and supporting capability differences. This approach requires a leader to really ask people for their opinion, as the leader *must have* what other people know and see and demonstrate that it's truly valued.

John Amaechi once again used the term 'energy expensive' in describing the vigilance needed to lead in this manner. As such, how you go about helping yourself and empowering your corporation, team or department as a leader is going to be intrinsically linked to your balance of Journey Motivators.

As you will have seen at the beginning of this chapter, the top performing leaders' views on empowerment resulted in the 20 points (as explained in Chapter 1) being allocated with 14 for ambiguous empowerment and 6 for unambiguous. Let's explore the two Journey Motivators in more depth.

JOURNEY MOTIVATOR 1
I ALLOW MY PEOPLE TO ASSUME ACCOUNTABILITY AND OWNERSHIP FOR SUCCESS AND WHAT THEY LEARN WHEN THINGS GO WRONG (AMBIGUOUS)

If you have children, you've likely told at least one toddler not to touch the stove. Unfortunately, some children will go ahead and do it anyway. A painful burn and much screaming ensues.

You, the parent, were correct. But you find aloe vera and a burn dressing anyway, and reassuringly hold the injured party until the crying stops.

Similar to the Resilience Destination Belief, Empowerment requires a culture of safety. After all, what point is there in telling – or ordering – your people to take accountability for something if you do not allow for the possibility of failure?

As we saw previously, in Chapter 3, a failure-fearing organization can quickly stumble and fall when faced with a new and unexpected challenge. But leaders who strongly relate to the Ambiguous Journey Motivator have a knack for folding failure seamlessly into their plans. As Michael Tobin told us: "Success isn't permanent and failure doesn't exist. You simply get up one more time than you've been knocked down."

Leaders like Michael understand the words of poet Samuel Beckett,[103] "Ever tried. Ever failed. No matter. Try again. Fail again. Fail better."

At home, Michael said, they have a rule: "You either succeeded in something or you learned something – there's no failure. We remove that fear of failure completely." Peter Lees voiced a similar thought: "We say you succeeded or you learned." Michael went even further: "If you've got a scenario where you're trying to get your team to push an envelope to do something that hasn't been done before, they're going to get it wrong. If they're not getting it wrong, they're not pushing the envelope enough because they're only going to get to the zones that have been tried and tested."

Well-suited to the project-based workflow that dominates today's corporations, this leader is a caring, nurturing parent rather than a chieftain. When beginning a project, the objective is scoped out with the team present and involved. The leader explores the terrain ahead and the course the others will face, and then hands the project over to their empowered team. Karen Penney puts it like this: "I love delegation, it's the best thing ever! How do people learn if they don't get the chance to do it? It might go wrong, but you are the leader and you have to judge how to play it. You cannot do it all yourself."

Watching from afar with a careful eye, but allowing their team to traverse the terrain, leaders who strongly relate to this Journey Motivator believe that their people should learn from these experiences and mistakes. These leaders are also excellent at balancing the many leadership dilemmas in their day-to-day work. They build close relationships with people, all while keeping a suitable distance yet leading them. They stay in the background, trusting people, yet they keep *an eagle eye* on what is happening.

CONFRONTING LIFE'S UNCERTAINTIES

Encouraging their people to confront life's inequities and uncertainties, these leaders waste no attention on doubt. What they must be wary of, however, are those less confident than themselves. When an overly cautious team is left to fail, or succeed, alone, they can frequently doubt and question a leader and their role. In fact, some rowdier team members may even question the role of leadership at all.

The duty of the leader, therefore, is to balance their ambiguous empowerment with unambiguous structures. This can also be closely linked to Google's research into high performing teams as part of 'Project Aristotle'. The research identified five key dynamics that set successful teams apart from the other teams at Google. The top dynamic was that of 'Psychological Safety',[104] or the ability to take risks without feeling insecure or embarrassed.

TEACH, DON'T TELL

Duke CE has for years worked with medical teams including at Johns Hopkins Hospital in Baltimore, Maryland, helping leaders understand the power of 'teach, don't tell'. Johns Hopkins has recently been ranked one of the top hospitals in the US – its 2019-2020 ranking is number three in the nation[105] – due in part to a culture that requires high productivity and efficiency.

In this risky and demanding environment, leaders needed to accelerate learning, productivity and mastery of skills, and improve outcomes by following a simple behavioural philosophy and set of principles governing the way they interact with their teams.

The three primary principles the hospital successfully implemented and adopted were:

1. **Teach, Don't Tell**: the use of questions and inquiry to teach junior doctors, rather than just providing them with the answer, or solving the issue for them.
2. **Point of the Wedge**: the practice of pushing responsibility, combined with support, to a less-experienced team member in order to increase teaching, learning and development.
3. **Own the Patient**: a heightened sense of accountability and motivation for team members in delivering quality 'customer' service.

Benefits of this approach can be seen in the diagram overleaf.

THE LEADER'S SECRET CODE

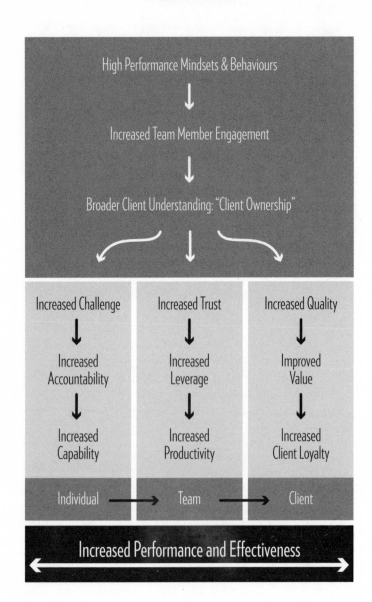

JOURNEY MOTIVATOR 2
I BELIEVE IN PROVIDING MY PEOPLE WITH CLEAR BOUNDARIES AS TO THE LIMIT/EXTENT OF DECISION-MAKING AND ACTION (UNAMBIGUOUS)

The Unambiguous Leader defines and specifies in detail the boundaries and daubs the 'red lines', making clear that the team may go *this far*, but no further, on their own. This leader is an enforcer (as opposed to Journey Motivator 1's 'enabler') and is proactive, clear and direct.

His or her behaviour will often be described as:

- Controlling/dominant
- Distrustful
- Independent
- Powerful
- Clear.

At their worst, Unambiguous Leaders hold leashes around their teams' necks. The leash is only so long and if the team tries to extend beyond, they will 'choke'. A disempowered, micro-managed, strangled team forfeits control to the leader.

People who must follow these leaders quickly lose heart and cease participating. And you can forget about them making a contribution.

In moderation, however, there is something of value in the Unambiguous Leader. This is because many people look to leadership for guidance and an understanding of their place – and their safety – within an organization.

THE LEADER'S SECRET CODE

Best suited to larger organizations, where old processes and firm structures require careful handling, the balance of Journey Motivator 2 and Journey Motivator 1 provides teams with autonomy, but psychological safety as well. (Again, this aligns with Google's Project Aristotle.)[106]

TIRED OLD TROPES

Author and media executive Arianna Huffington of *The Huffington Post* tells the story of how a lack of boundaries led to her overworking and taking a traumatic fall in her office.[107] At the time, she said, she'd bought into the old trope that burnout was the necessary price of success ... until she fainted from exhaustion, smashed her head into her desk and broke a cheekbone. The incident led her to create boundaries around the need for rest.

Along those lines, Twitter and Square co-founder and CEO Jack Dorsey has a consistent, uninterrupted morning routine of unplugging himself from the world for an hour, during which he walks five miles to his office, giving him clarity and focus for the day ahead.[108]

For an ambitious business leader on the go, it can be challenging to grow your company while attempting to discern and prioritize all of the tasks that are thrown your way each day. However, every leader eventually has a moment of truth when the lack of clear and defined boundaries creates major conflicts, both personally and professionally.

There are four boundaries you must consider if you want to grow as an effective and productive leader:

1. **Time Boundaries**

   Carol Sankar says that she used to be guilty of accepting every call, responding to every email and attending every networking event. After months of saying yes to everything, she realized that she was not taking care of herself. The feelings of fatigue and exhaustion began to take a toll that was a clear sign of a need for change.[109]

   When you are in control of your time, you prioritize tasks on the basis of importance. It is essential to create time boundaries so you can protect your personal time as well. It is time to turn it off. One CEO we spoke with simply abandoned emails altogether. We asked him how it was going. "Work in progress," he replied.

   Realistically, every task and request is not a priority.[110] The ability to say 'no' more often is a consistent challenge for a leader, especially those within the entrepreneurial, start-up environment.

2. **Financial Boundaries**

   Everyone is shopping for the best deal, but your company must always focus on becoming the best solution, which may come at a premium. One of the boundaries you must establish up front is a financial boundary.[111]

   We receive hundreds of message requests each week, via various social media platforms, asking for advice and counsel. Do you have 20 minutes to look over something? What's your take on this quick how-to question? Frankly, we're unable to respond to most of these without a fee commitment ... as it of course should be for a consultative business.

Hence, the financial barrier is also honouring your time boundaries.

3. **Social Media Boundaries**

Do you have too many notifications popping up on your phone? How many times per day are you scrolling through your timeline? How many IGTV (Instagram) or Facebook Live sessions are you watching during the day?

It is essential to set specific times throughout the day to check your social media feed, instead of coming to a dead stop every time an alert goes off. Our rule of thumb: check in three times a day – for 15-20 minutes each – morning, noon and night. That gives you a total of approximately one hour of social media time daily, segmented into three chunks. This goes a long way toward limiting the constant distraction and creates support for your tribe, without interrupting productivity.[112]

4. **Personal Time and Recharging Boundaries**

Make clear, non-negotiable personal time and physical rest a priority. Whether it's making time to spend with family or a dinner date with friends, make it a weekly priority. You need time to unwind and refuel in order to remain effective.

Call it 'unplugging from the matrix'. Every workaholic needs to have fun once in a while, and setting aside time to prioritize others is part of the growth process. Spend time having unfiltered fun and laughter and make sure your team is aware that you are not available, unless it is an emergency.

On the subject of laughter, it has become central to the way Bruce Daisley leads and the culture that he creates. He applies this in his leadership role at Twitter, in the books he writes and the podcasts he creates. "The thing I've always enjoyed, and the reason why I wanted to do something about work culture, is that I enjoy the sound of laughter at work," he told us. "I was always inspired by the importance of laughter and I found there's loads of science about laughter."

He continued: "A good day at work is sort of laughing all day – laughing and being around people who are fun to be around, inspiring to be around. There's not a lot of internal politics here; people are pretty straight-forward. My bosses have been the most brilliant people, so the good humour and the gratitude for life has always extended upwards to my bosses."

Chris Newitt shares that view. "Every meeting should have one good laugh," he told us. "We spend too much time at work, so if you're not having a laugh you are not going to get the best out of your team." James Knight told us a similar story: "I used to really enjoy looking at ways we could welcome people to a team, and it was just simple things. So rather than have a welcoming drinks night we go for a welcoming run on the beach – a race across this beach, about five miles, and we would finish at a waterfall. All the new lads would jump in the waterfall and then tell a story in front of the whole company."

MY EMPOWERMENT REVIEW

Below are some questions relating to the Destination Belief of Empowerment. Find a quiet place, contemplate the questions and write down your responses. Better still, verbalize them out loud. Doing so will move you along on the journey of applying The Leader's Secret Code.

Q1. Am I setting expectations clearly? Does everyone understand the vision and goals? Am I then allowing my people to deliver the results?

Q2. Do my people hear from me like a sudden lightning strike (incisive strike and that's it), or like rolling thunder (more of a constant rumbling presence)? What do I want to keep the same, or change? (Think about this in the context of the balance of logos, ethos and pathos.)

Q3. Do I ask questions rather than make statements about 'how I would do something' or 'what I did in the past'? Far better to inquire as to 'What was your intention when you took that decision?' as opposed to, 'That was a really stupid idea'!

Q4. How well do I listen … really listen?

Q5. Do I give my people enough of my time? Empowerment is not another word for 'ignoring'.

WHAT'S IN THE MIND?

The psychologist says ...

Many people work in environments that are dominated by 'stick and carrot' motivation: do well and you'll get a reward ... but do badly and you'll be punished. However, with this approach the fulfilment of doing a job well often gets dismissed in the fight for praise. We know from many years of research that employees perform better when they are motivated, but what about empowered?

In the 2011 edition of his book, *Drive*, Daniel Pink sets out a new vision for workplace motivation, which he labels "Motivation 3.0."[113] Pink's theory is drawn from research undertaken by psychologists Harry Harlow and Edward Deci in 1971. They discovered that rewards can fail to improve people's engagement with tasks and may even damage it. Another study was carried out by professors at MIT in 2017 and recorded similar findings. Pink argues that traditional 'carrot and stick' approaches to motivation are becoming outdated, and do not adequately address the needs of the creative and innovative workplaces of today. According to Pink, there are three elements which empower employees: autonomy, mastery and purpose.

AUTONOMY

Autonomy is the desire to direct your own life and work. To be fully motivated, you must be able to control what you do, when you do it and who you do it with. According to Pink, autonomy motivates us to think creatively without needing to conform to strict workplace rules. By rethinking traditional governance – regular office hours, dress codes,

targets and so on – organizations can increase staff autonomy, build trust and improve innovation and creativity
through letting employees create their own boundaries.
Empowerment by autonomy is being used more often
in organizations, for example through the use of out-
come-based working. This is result-based, focusing on the
outputs, quality or outcomes. Employees have autonomy
to work the hours they wish or need in order to deliver
those results. This empowers employees to have autonomy
over their working hours, place of work and so on as long
as they deliver the results.

MASTERY

Mastery is the urge to get better and better at something
that matters. If you or your people are motivated by mastery, you'll likely see your potential as being unlimited and
you'll constantly seek to improve your skills through continued learning.

PURPOSE

This is the yearning to do what we do in the service of
something larger than ourselves. People may become dis-
engaged and demotivated at work if they don't understand,
or can't invest in, the 'bigger picture'. Too much bigger
picture can make employees feel like it is all a dream, but
it is important they believe they have some accountability
and ownership for future success.

Making the change to a way of working that empowers employees to assume accountability for success can
be daunting. Here are a few ways you can start to change
the culture to adopt a degree of empowerment within
your teams:

- Allow people to organize their own time; focus on the desired outputs and results rather than when the time is spent or what time is spent working on the task at hand.
- Release autonomy to others by allowing people to set their own goals; you can offer advice on what these should look like, or how they should align to the overall business objectives, but allowing people the autonomy to create them with their own language and measures will drive success toward achieving them.
- Promote collaboration amongst your own team members, but also employees from other teams or business units. 'Hot desking' (where people have no fixed desk and can sit in a different place each day) is a good way to facilitate this. It enables people to choose who they work with and promotes knowledge sharing between members of different teams.

THE LAST WORD ON EMPOWERMENT

EMPOWERMENT, OPRAH-STYLE

It would be fair to say that Oprah Winfrey is African American empowerment in human form. One could also say that Oprah is the epitome of women's empowerment. But it would probably be most accurate to say that Oprah is the embodiment of *human* empowerment. Full stop.

Born into poverty in rural Mississippi to a teen single mother, and herself pregnant at 14 by an abuser (her baby boy died in infancy), Oprah's start was as tough as they come.

Today, of course, she is among the most influential women in the world, hailed as one of the greatest black philanthropists in American history. The media mogul, actress, talk show host and personal-development advocate has empowered hundreds of thousands of people – women, men, black, white, young and old – to make the most of their lives.

Oprah's balance of the Ambiguous and Unambiguous Journey Motivators has developed her understanding of 'empowerment'. True empowerment, she has said, comes in the form of making your own personal decision on how best to use your talents to be of service to others.

This is especially important to leaders; what you share of your own talents leads to a much wider circle of empowerment for others. Oprah encourages leaders to work at discovering how they can use everything they've been given – all their talents and experience as a person – to be of greater service than just to themselves.

This means giving to and sharing with the team the very best of yourself. Your time, your understandings and a real, authentic sense of empowerment comes from making this decision and following it through.

"Your legacy," Oprah said, "is every life you touch."[114]

Empowering your team means that your footprint remains long after 'the doing is done'.

CHAPTER
NINE

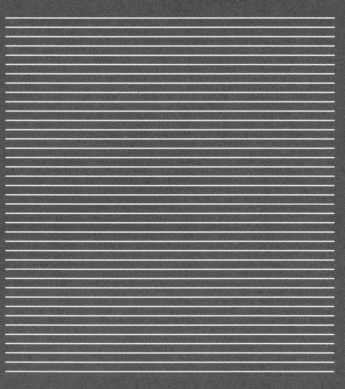

FULFILMENT

Destination Belief
I am most fulfilled when I am successful (Fulfilment)

Journey behaviours   Journey behaviours

Journey Motivator 1
The extent to which you believe fulfilment comes through being recognised for your personal and organizational success

Journey Motivator 2
The degree to which your sense of fulfilment derives from feelings of communal connection and success with those you lead

Achievement   Affiliation

1   **19**

Described as a sense of contentment following the achievement of expectations or desires, fulfilment is the final part of The Leader's Secret Code.

Fulfilment is a key tool for leaders in motivating themselves and others, as it accompanies the transition to new goals and objectives for the company and attention turns to a new set of criteria. As such, it is possibly the hardest of all the Destination Beliefs to achieve.

Leadership is understanding that we are all inspired to contribute our gifts toward something greater than ourselves and we experience fulfilment as we do. Many organizations understand the throughflow of fulfilment via purpose, culture and what the organization values.

As Michael Tobin told us: "There was a point where I had to come to terms with who I was and what I wanted. So, I had to be honest with myself, take the mask off and actually ask myself, *why are you doing this?*"

It comes as no surprise that all leaders we interviewed demonstrated a burning desire to be successful and a belief that success begets both professional and personal fulfilment. What you may not expect (we didn't) was that a significant number of our leaders disagreed on what constituted 'the path to fulfilment'. Some believe they achieve success when they're recognized for great achievement, while others staunchly advocate the triumph of their community, team and company – bringing others into the spotlight of success.

PURSUIT OF A BETTER LIFE

When we spoke to Tamara Rojo, it was clear that fulfilment worked for her on multiple levels. As we've described, Tamara from a very young age viewed ballet as her perfect oasis – it allowed her to be herself through movement. In her Artistic Director role she fell in love with helping her dancers in the pursuit of "wanting to make life better, not just make beautiful ballet".

She blossoms as she talks of her belief that "the life of a man or woman has purpose that is bigger than their own self-satisfaction." She truly believes that ballet has the power to break barriers and "move people to an emotional experience, not just an intellectual experience".

It is hard to be successful in all aspects of leadership – there's growing evidence that this is empirically true. For example, Gallup's 2008 book, *Strengths Based Leadership*,[115] summarized decades of the consulting firm's research on leaders and leadership around the world. One of the key findings was that "the best leaders are not well rounded, the best teams are". It goes on to state that the best leaders therefore surround themselves with the right people and build on each person's strengths.

Edgecumbe Consulting,[116] in conducting leadership assessments of thousands of leaders from many different countries, reached similar conclusions. Edgecumbe noted that no leader, from these thousands, was world-class in all the aspects of leadership it scrutinized. They joke that this is either the world's worst sampling error or a significant finding in its own right! Further evidence suggests it is the latter.

Strategic and operational?

	Neutral or worse	Effectively	Very effectively
Very effectively	1%	2%	8%
Effectively	12%	23%	4%
Neutral or worse	35%	14%	1%

Executes strategy

Develops strategy and identity with vision

Further evidence comes from studies that have unwittingly turned up consistent supportive data.

PwC, for example, in its 2013 study[117] of 700 executives from around the world, asked respondents to rate managers/leaders on different aspects of their performance and capability. Two questions asked how well the individual develops strategy and identity with vision (strategic domain) and how well he or she executes strategy (operational domain). Only 8% were rated as doing both 'Very effectively' (see above matrix).

Keen-eyed observers may point out that the diagonal axis in this table contains two-thirds of the data, suggesting a positive correlation, but that's almost entirely due to the fact that it seems easy to do both poorly! This finding does not take into account the interpersonal domain, but the findings are consistent with our second proposition.

In 2017, CEB/Gartner reported in the *Harvard Business Review*[118] a three-year study of 9,000 leaders in 85 global companies. They assessed the executives' experience, and gauged their personality and performance on a variety of psychometric and '360-degree feedback' measures. In addition, they assessed the contexts in which the executives were operating.

AGILITY VS SPECIALIZATION

According to the researchers: "Two-thirds of the top-performing leaders in the study weren't particularly well-rounded; they were ... 'spiky', meaning that they excelled at a few specific capabilities but were not above average in all." From this they concluded: "Chasing managerial agility instead of allowing for specialization is ineffective."

There are also suggestions from personality and leadership research that personality characteristics work differently in different aspects of leadership. Openness helps in the strategic domain, but it can get in the way in the operational domain. The reason is that openness shows up as 'curiosity' strategically but can become 'distractibility' operationally. This suggests one way in which personality research supports the notion that it's hard to be world-class in all aspects of leadership.

For these reasons, findings suggest that rather than trying to be good in all areas, it may be better to be great in one or two and work with others who are great in other areas.

Steve Jobs famously quipped: "It doesn't make sense to hire smart people and tell them what to do; we hire smart people so they can tell us what to do."[119]

This removes the burden of *incipient perfectionism* – and the tendency to invest all of one's developmental effort into trying to eliminate limitations – when it may be much more effective to further develop strengths. Indeed, few managers make it to the top of large organizations by being 'okay' at everything. They usually make it to the C Suite by being outstanding at one or two things ... and being for-given for others.

And this leads us to our last Destination Belief, which concerns success. It goes to the existential question of what you want to achieve and what you feel once you've achieved it.

JOURNEY MOTIVATOR 1
I AM FULFILLED WHEN I AM RECOGNIZED FOR MY PERSONAL AND ORGANIZATIONAL SUCCESS (ACHIEVEMENT)

"Recognition is everything to me," says Michael Tobin. "It's big."

Well, who doesn't want a healthy dose of love praise? You know, a high five here or a powerful nod there.

Individualism – defined as valuing interests of the individual over those of the state or a social group – is a growing trend. In their book, *Leadership 2030: The Six Megatrends You Need to Understand to Lead Your Company into the Future*,[120] authors Georg Vielmetter and Yvonne Sell suggest that individualism is poised to challenge, and inevitably change, leadership styles of the future. And its impact is already being felt.

Millennials have started to enter the workforce and anyone who's had to manage these new recruits has seen not only a different work ethic, but also an altogether different approach to their careers, company loyalty and so much more.

Individualism is part of a Millennial's DNA, and it's powerfully driven and enhanced by digitization. As industries succumb to game-changing technologies, the full impact of individualization on companies and brands becomes evident. One size no longer fits all.

In a business that wants to promote individualism, managers largely allow employees to look after their own work.

Workers are given freedom to explore new ways of completing basic procedures or projects, using empowerment (our previous Destination Belief). Unless someone presents a threat, or otherwise isn't performing up to snuff, they are afforded a significant degree of privacy. Everyone gets a chance to voice individual opinions, open debate is allowed and management responds readily to requests for personal time.

A MACHIAVELLIAN BENT

Achievement-oriented leaders who nurture a culture of individualism are often described as being:

- Competitive
- Driven
- Machiavellian
- Strong willed
- Independent.

Although individualism can promote innovation, it can understandably hinder cooperation. In the long run, this sometimes means that productivity suffers and conflicts increase. Lack of productivity can decrease overall revenue and conflicts may cost money to resolve. Individualism also can create a tense work environment if people are too rigid in their ideals.

However, a key benefit to promoting individualism is that employees have a high level of personal responsibility. That is, they cannot freeload, assuming that others would even be willing to pick up the slack. Individualism also creates a degree of healthy competition, as each person can demonstrate his own skills and talents and rise in the ranks accordingly. As part of this competitive dynamic, workers may exhibit great amounts of innovation and creativity as they strive to shine. In such a setting, they also may find unique solutions to conflicts that arise.

Social scientist and opinion researcher Ron Inglehart[121] has been carrying out global values surveys for the past 35 years. Among his most robust findings, explored in a series of books over the past two decades, is a universal, secular trend toward increasing individualism. The United States, 'land of the free and home of the brave', is the leader in this trend. But individualism is on the rise globally as well, spanning national and socio-cultural boundaries.

Thinking about the dialectic between individualism and collectivism, we cannot deny the dangers of too much individualism: emphasis on entitlement over social responsibility, creeping narcissism and a selfish indifference to the needs of others. But these pale in comparison to the oppressiveness of excessive collectivism. The fall of Communism stands as the 20th century's most obvious turn away from collectivism.

But there are less obvious data points as well: consider the *hikikomori*, for example, the 1.5 million young people in Japan who will not leave their bedrooms.[122]

UNWILLING TO PLAY THE GAME

In *Shutting Out the Sun*, Michael Zielenziger,[123] a journalist who spent nine years reporting from Japan for *Reuters*, argues that these young people, mostly male, are not all autistic. They are not video game addicts. They're not classic agoraphobes, and they're not crazy. If airlifted out of Japan to places like Hong Kong, Vancouver or New York, many thrive.

But in Japan – with its strong, homogeneous culture that stresses society's needs over the individual's – they're simply unwilling to play the collectivist game. They drop out. Their parents, unwilling to *lose face* by openly acknowledging their children's asocial behaviour, end up enabling their reclusiveness.

Businesses often promote collectivism because of the advantages that teamwork provides. For some companies that are highly dependent on creativity, complete elimination of individualism in the workplace is not necessarily desirable. Many operate with a combination of collective and individualistic philosophies, effectively measuring individual performance in the context of group work.

JOURNEY MOTIVATOR 2
I AM FULFILLED WHEN I EXPERIENCE COMMUNAL CONNECTION AND SUCCESS WITH THOSE I LEAD (AFFILIATION)

Most leaders relate to the notion that individual team members' personal fulfilment enhances overall organizational performance. Those who are fulfilled by shared successes thrive on teamwork, empowerment, joint ownership and accountability.

The qualities and behaviours associated with this Journey Motivator include:
- Good at prioritizing
- Good listening skills
- Co-operative/collaborative
- Empowering.

These leaders make time to listen to, identify, discuss and nurture the aspirations and desires of the individuals in the team. They take the necessary steps to fulfil them through meaningful rewards for attainment of milestones toward company goals. They epitomize the win-win scenario.

As leaders who inspire the team to achieve a high level of productivity, these individuals engender a sense of unwavering loyalty and are typically magnanimous and selfless in the office. They carefully explain employees' vested interest in hitting milestones and goals, in a way that motivates each individual and the team as a whole.

Through this, leaders who strongly relate to Journey Motivator 2 gain personal fulfilment. As Bruce Daisley told us: "I like giving people the spotlight. I'll never be in the centre of the front row in a group picture." He added: "I don't have a car, I don't own a watch. I bought a flat once. I am not remotely interested in status. Experiences matter to me."

Fear – or rather, the lack thereof – plays an important part in a leader's fulfilment here as well. When playing for a team, eliminating or minimizing repercussions opens the door to personal fulfilment, optimal performance and winning results ... for all parties, without the fear of failure snapping at their heels.

FOSTERING A SAFE ENVIRONMENT

This is a key, defining characteristic of this Journey Motivator: the fostering of an environment that is 'safe' for the team. It provides a place where everyone can comfortably share and discuss their needs and concerns. In team meetings and one-on-one sessions, a leader explores the impact that individuals' work has on the company. This shows people how important they are and spotlights contributions they make to the overall success or failure of the group.

For this reason, we were not surprised to learn that top-performing leaders, when assessed, valued fulfilment through affiliation to a much higher degree than fulfilment through achievement (19 points versus 1 point, using the approach outlined in Chapter 1).

People, it has been said, have long been promoted to their level of incompetence. As they are generally talented, bright and motivated people, it's unlikely that such a high percentage of them were promoted beyond their ability.

What's actually going on is that these people are making a common, very easy to understand mistake. When they got into their new leadership positions, they kept doing all the things that got them there. They didn't realize that leadership is a different sort of thing than management and, even more significantly, it's not synonymous with being an individual contributor.

Much of the time, people reach positions of formal leadership because they've proven themselves to be fantastic individual contributors. For instance, they did excellent work coding pages for the website (an individual contributor task), and as a result were promoted to head up the whole web division (a leadership task).

They act like an individual contributor in a leadership role and end up doing all the wrong things. They probably even did *all the wrong things* extremely well, since it was likely their capacity for individual contribution that propelled them into the leadership ranks. But since they were doing the wrong things, it backfired and undermined their effectiveness in the more senior role.

Many of the leadership interventions we've orchestrated have focused on the individual's ability (or inability) to transition between leadership styles. For example, this has involved moving from technical leadership to adaptive leadership. This requires leaders to shift away from only giving clear direction and answers, to helping others to learn and adapt ... without losing the right to give clear directions and answers on non-negotiables.

At the higher levels of an organization, it's about a whole lot more than your ability to personally *do* the work. Rather, your primary role is now to set direction, align your team, inspire enthusiasm and give thought to the direction of the whole organization. *That* is a true enterprise leader.

If you remain focused on *doing* the work yourself – acting like another member of the team, handling another equally-weighted chunk of work that everyone else is doing – you're neglecting the things that you're really in your role to do. If you keep trying to do the sorts of things you did as an individual contributor, you simply won't have time to lead at all.

LEADING ... AND CONTRIBUTING

That's the main take-away here: start leading *in addition to* continuing to act as an individual contributor.

If you're consumed with trying to carry out your old functional responsibilities, your individual contribution tasks will interfere with your leadership tasks. It's necessary to stop mucking around in most of your former 'down in the weeds' activities in order to be able to lead.

There is a range here, of course. It's not that the leader has no responsibilities as an individual contributor, but his or her primary area of focus absolutely must be *being a leader.*

There are a few core things you need to stop doing – and things you need to do – in order to succeed at the executive level. Let's explore that for a moment.

Executive leadership requires setting down responsibility for few results and picking up accountability for many results.

To be 'responsible' for something is to be involved in the details. You're either doing it directly or closely involved in directing those who are. Obviously, this doesn't scale – if you are closely involved in the details of things, you won't have the time to deal with a lot of things.

To be 'accountable', on the other hand, is to be answerable for the results that other people (your team members) achieve. Since you aren't still down in the weeds of doing things, this enables you can be accountable for many things, which is exactly what any leadership role requires.

A leader needs to accomplish *more* than they did as an individual contributor, not less ... but in different ways. When you lead, your efforts are multiplied through the influence you have on the contributions of others. Thus, the leader needs to spend less time on individual projects and more time working across the scope of the organization.

MY FULFILMENT REVIEW

Below are some questions relating to the Destination Belief of Fulfilment. Find a quiet place, contemplate the questions and write down your responses. Better still, verbalize them out loud. Doing so will move you along on the journey of applying The Leader's Secret Code.

Q1. To what extent do you consider your own personal and professional needs above those of others in your organization?

Q2. How important is being recognised for what you have achieved to you?

Q3. How much effort do you put into getting to know your people? What examples can you think of?

Q4. Are you happy with your life and career as it is now? If yes, why is that? If no, what will you change?

Q5. What is your passion? Why?

WHAT'S IN THE MIND?

The psychologist says ...

Described as a sense of contentment following the achievement of expectations or desires, fulfilment is a key tool for leaders in motivating themselves and others. Workplace motivation can be a difficult and complex subject for leaders and individuals themselves, but it's still important to understand the basics. Motivation can be thought of as a continuum, with values and rewards represented by intrinsic (internal) elements at one end, and by extrinsic (external) factors at the other.

Intrinsic motivation means we are motivated by rewards that are largely intangible. This means we place more value on outcomes that are sourced from within, rather than from external factors. The motivation to engage in a behaviour arises from within the individual because it is naturally satisfying to you and is often linked to enjoyment in our work. Intrinsic motivation comes from 'within' and leaders need to establish how to promote and support intrinsic motivation in their people. How do you ensure that the value, achievements and efforts of employees are fully and fairly recognized?

Extrinsic motivation refers to behaviour that is driven by external rewards such as money, fame, grades and praise. This type of motivation arises from outside the individual, as opposed to intrinsic motivation, which originates inside. We are also motivated to perform by things or factors which come from other people or organizations other than oneself. Examples of extrinsic motivation include salary, security, benefits, the physical work environment and the conditions of work (shift patterns, office layout, etc.) In some cases, some factors relating to the motivators are outside the control of a line manager (for example, the office in which your team works in has no windows) and are more often determined at an organizational level.

Nonetheless, effective managers should be supportive of colleagues motivated by extrinsic factors and will acknowledge this and be creative in their thinking.

The continuum of motivation, with intrinsic at one end and extrinsic at the other, can map to the Journey Motivators of fulfilment which is also a continuum. At one end we find some people motivated by tangible, extrinsic benefits, such as salary and as a leader, you may be motivated by the extent to which you feel recognised for your personal and organizational success. Others may be motivated by factors at the opposite end of the spectrum. These people tend to forego the tangible rewards of monetary benefits, in favour of intrinsic or self-satisfaction, and this fulfilment as a leader may come from feelings of communal connection, success of those you lead or success as a team.

To gain the most from the basics of motivation, it's best to remember that people can easily move along any continuum. Rather than considering these motivational factors as opposites, we need to remind ourselves that most people are motivated by a combination of the two, not simply one or the other. And that such motivation is also influenced by a number of other complex, social and economic factors, such as age, family status and so on, not to mention certain variables that are completely outside of one's control.

THE LAST WORD
ON FULFILMENT

FROM HERO TO ZERO:
WHEN PERSONAL ACHIEVEMENT MEANS
MORE THAN COLLECTIVE SUCCESS

Jack Jones managed one of his country's leading rugby
teams. Jack had enjoyed an illustrious managerial career,
with a cabinet full of trophies won at the highest level.
He'd stopped counting once they numbered in excess of
20. Famous in his Welsh homeland and across the world
of rugby for his tactical mind and knowledge of the
game, his charisma was also legendary. True, he could be
somewhat brusque, even abrasive, but it had done him no
harm. Jack Jones had it all.

Although he was lauded in rugby circles, even called
'iconic', Jack was dissatisfied. He could not ignore the
fact that he had not managed the country's biggest, most
successful club. He had tried and failed to land the top-
club job once before. Having got over his disappoint-
ment he went on to win more trophies and the next time
his dream job became available Jack was ready, his cre-
dentials impeccable.

In fact, he was gratified when the biggest club in the
country came knocking at his door. After a suitable period
and hard contract negotiation, Jack accepted his 'coronation' with aplomb. The lights of the TV crews and the
flashes from the cameras were bright as the club's chief
executive announced that in Jack, "We have got our man.

This rugby club is known and admired worldwide. We are honoured to have Jack and I know that Jack is honoured to be at this club, with its mystique, its reputation, its romance!"

Jack's reign started well. His individualistic leadership style provided short-term success: winning the league in his first season and achieving a 60% win-rate in his second. He felt fulfilled by the added recognition and personal and organizational success which came his way (Achievement).

A REVERSAL OF FORTUNE

Yet, just two years into his tenure, Jack's dream turned into a nightmare. The team grew tired of his abrasive and distant style. A lack of personal connection created a vacuum which was filled with rumblings of dressing room discontent. That kind of familiarity with the players did not appeal to Jack. He believed that as long as they continued to enjoy success that in itself was enough to ensure the loyalty of the team. He was wrong.

Halfway through his third season, the club he had dreamed of managing fired him unceremoniously.

The achiever's dreams – Jack Jones' dreams – disintegrated into despair and discord. The glittering career punctuated by victories left, right and centre meant nothing. There were no offers of employment forthcoming, for no executive board wished to risk a repeat of this sorry tale. The world of rugby – and of sport in general – learned that the Achievement Journey Motivator must be carefully balanced with that of Affiliation if Fulfilment is to be achieved.

The late, great Arthur Ashe – best known as the only black man ever to win the men's singles tennis titles at Wimbledon, the US Open and the Australian Open – said,

"Success is a journey, not a destination. The doing is more important than the outcome."

If only Joe had heeded those words of wisdom.

CHAPTER
TEN

UNLOCKING
YOUR CODE

Through our exhaustive study of high-performing leaders, spanning organizations of all sorts worldwide, we can reveal that the key to successful leadership lies in 7 Destination Beliefs and 14 Journey Beliefs.

We also now understand that although every high-performing leader holds many Journey Beliefs, the secret of top performers is that they hold a *specific combination of intensity of each Journey Belief.*

This optimal balance makes up The Leader's Secret Code.

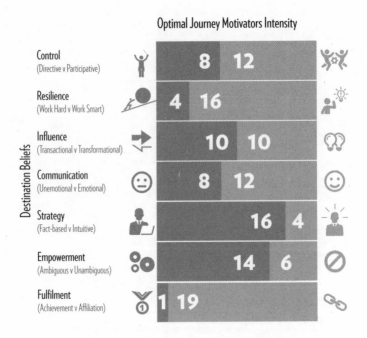

Optimal Journey Motivators Intensity

Your own balance of intensity may align closely to this, or it may be somewhat different. Only you will know what your personal mix is and it's likely that you'll only come to your conclusions after considerable reflection ... and perhaps a long and arduous process of trial and error.

What we uncovered in this study emerged through considerable analysis of the language used by leaders in response to our questions, and their behavioural and motivational preferences.

In the next few pages we reveal how you, holding this book, can unlock your beliefs and use The Leader's Secret Code to perform at your best. We can infer from our previous study – into the characteristics and behaviours that drive fulfilment and success for salespeople – that the top -performing leaders succeed in large part because their beliefs drive them to think and behave in ways that support their intensity of belief.

Congruence, it seems, is a powerful element that informs both the individual and those they lead.

WHERE DO YOUR PROCLIVITIES LIE?

Now that you have discovered The Leader's Secret Code, it is time to ask yourself what you believe in. Where do your proclivities for each Journey Motivator lie?

If you've taken the time to reflect and answer the questions in this book's motivation reviews, it is likely that you already understand your relationship with each Destination Belief and each Journey Motivator. If you have yet to do this, go back and do it ... now. Your legacy as a leader will thank you for it.

Once you have acquired the necessary self-knowledge, and with the insights we have laid out for you, you are ready to answer the final question: Do I want to be a better leader?

Consider:

1. Why and how might The Leader's Secret Code be important and make a difference to my team?

2. Where does my team's balance of Journey Motivators lie? Where is it relative to that of the top-performing leaders?

3. Is there something I can do to enable a shift in my team's motivational balance to the optimal balance? What help do I need from other leaders and stakeholders?

Nothing – not a meaningful mission, powerful purpose, high pay cheque or forward-thinking vision – is going to help your team be the best they can be if they do not believe certain things about themselves. And you are the one who can take them there. The Leader's Secret Code is the guide to bringing out your leadership's full potential.

TAKING THE NEXT STEP

1. Reflect on and write down your own distribution of Journey Motivators.

2. Select a Destination Belief from The Code that you'd like to 'try on'. The most effective way to do this is to thumb through each chapter in this book while you ask yourself the following questions:
   - What do I want to achieve for myself?
   - What do I want to achieve for my team?
   - What would it be like to master this Destination Belief?
   - What might happen when I achieve the optimal view of this belief?
   - What is it that would make the difference I want to see and experience for myself?

3. Compare the optimum balance of Journey Motivators we have presented for your chosen Destination Belief with your own sense of the 'best-for-you' balance.

4. Now, think of a different situation – a time when you were absolutely brilliant. What was that like? Where were you? What was happening? What were you doing that was so remarkable? What were others around you seeing, hearing and feeling as they experienced your brilliance? We call this process 'association'. You are associating with a time when

you demonstrated the very attributes, skills, talents and behaviours that you're seeking to recapture now. Isn't it interesting that we discover that we can already do and be what we think we're missing?

5. As you continue to connect or associate with that time when you were being brilliant, you can help yourself to hold the feeling. We call this 'anchoring'. You might touch your wedding ring or your watch as you associate with the feelings, or you might close your eyes. Sometime, as you anchor, the feelings might dissipate. If so, this is normal – just stop the anchoring process, pause and re-associate in a moment or two. Sometimes it can take several 'trying-on sessions' to anchor successfully.

6. When you're happy that you are associating fully with the time when you were being brilliant – when you *believe deep down* that you are in fact brilliant – re-connect with the Destination Belief. Now, allow yourself to explore:
   • Your environment – where you are and what it is like
   • How you are behaving – what you're saying and doing that shows clearly that you are being brilliant or surprising yourself
   • What talents you are displaying in this moment
   • What is important to you, and how knowing this is supporting your behaviours and talents
   • How being like this affects your appreciation of yourself. Take stock of what is shifting, moving, evolving

- What wider impact you are now having. Perhaps as you're being brilliant you are becoming a role model for others ... or maybe you're actually setting the tone for how business can be conducted across your entire industry.

It is important to keep repeating this process – this is how we adopt a cycle of continuous learning and growth.

Many of the Iconics we spoke with worked proactively on the process of continual learning. Learning is the single best investment of our time that we can make. As Gandhi said: "Live as if you were to die tomorrow. Learn as if you were to live forever."

Lifelong learning is something that Bruce Daisley is passionate about. He talks about not working in the evening, but he spends that time researching those fascinating and accomplished people he'll be interviewing for his podcasts. He reads academic studies, much to the surprise of the authors he later interviews. As noted earlier, he was delighted when he established that there is a science behind laughter. He has achieved so much, and yet he is planning to pursue a Masters in Psychology and Neuroscience.

Through it all, Bruce told us, "I'm a very cheerful person." He then paused for a moment before continuing: "No, I should qualify that. I'm a very sort of *critical but cheerful* person. I love pop music. I can't tell you how happy it makes me to be learning stuff. I love doing stuff. Okay, I'll tell you what, *I'm a very active person*, right?"

Over time, often imperceptibly, our beliefs about ourselves change. As our beliefs alter, so do our behaviours. We become the embodiment of our new beliefs. In the end, this happens because we have given ourselves permission to be different.

BECOME A 'MODELLER'

"By appreciation, we make excellence in others our own property."

— Voltaire, 1694–1778

Once you have tried things on in the Destination Belief 'dressing room' – and have accepted your newfound ability to change your beliefs, and thus change your behaviour – it is time to become the leader you truly aspire to be.

Top performers are, by their very nature, important role models. The Iconic leaders we've highlighted throughout this book have provided wonderful examples of how they apply powerful beliefs and motivations to give themselves that special combination that supports their collective success.

They have discovered for themselves the perfect balance between the two Journey Motivators within each Destination Belief – a balance that enables them to perform at the top of their game. Each of them understood that the alternative to this worldview was to be avoided at all costs, for as the old Chinese proverb states: "The fish rots from the head down."

To capitalize on their combined insights, it's incumbent upon you to decide – here and now – to learn from role models and apply their techniques for yourself. When we adopt a behaviour other people display, we call it 'modelling'.

Anyone can model. In fact, throughout your life you will have been modelling other people, knowingly or subconsciously. It's how we learn and grow. You will have modelled your parents and may still do so; you'll have adopted gestures and expressions from your siblings and friends; you will have learned from your teachers; you will have picked up on how to perform tasks from colleagues at work. The list of people you will have modelled in your life is sure to be considerable.

All of us can pause to watch and listen to how other people operate. What we are inviting you to do, therefore, is to make modelling something that you do quite deliberately, with full awareness. You can add this information to what you learn about yourself as you live your daily life.

HOW TO MODEL IN SIX STEPS

1. Find your 'what' and 'who' and 'wow!'. What is one specific quality you observe in someone else that you want to adopt for yourself? For example, you may want to become a transformational leader and less of a transactional leader (see Chapter 5: Influence) and have admired how a colleague seems to have influence over others. That's a skill you want to emulate. Identify the effect their behaviour or talent has on you and others. What do you see, hear and feel? When you can do this, you will have found the 'wow!' factor.

2. Watch 'how'. Observe this model at work. Watch them talking to other people and the effect their behaviours have. Watch the way they move; perhaps they sit at the head of the conference table, or maybe they always sit in the middle. What is it about their combination of hand gestures, eye contact, tone of voice and use of humour that gives them that *special something* that makes them something special?

3. Ask them. In a quiet moment, invite your 'who' – your model – to picture themselves using the talent you have observed and ask them for their insights:

- Who and what are around you?
- What are you doing?
- What are you saying?
- What talents are you using?
- What are you feeling?
- What truly matters to you in this moment?
- How would you describe yourself?

Be very clear to your model that they can take their time in describing those qualities and behaviours, especially when they themselves may not be aware of the talents you've observed.

4. Do: Reflect upon what you've learned from your observations and your conversations. Then, step into your model's shoes, leaving behind any preconceptions you may hold. Assume that what they say and do is now the way *you* say and do. Now, feel it!

5. Evaluate: As you adopt the behaviours of your model, be 'fully present' and aware as you are modelling the new behaviour. Take note when aspects of what you are doing make a difference to you. Be prepared to discard something if it decidedly does not produce an improvement for you.

6. Adopt and Adapt: Allow the process, behaviour, language pattern – whatever it is that you have modelled – to become part of your identity. Internalize it, make it your own and put it to use in your interaction with others. This can take time, so give it the time required.

THE LAST, LAST WORD

With the foregoing guidance we come to the end of *The Leader's Secret Code*. In this final chapter we have presented ways to apply the unlocking of your own leader's code, through the evaluation and reframing of your own beliefs and the modelling of excellence in others. Our study has been designed to be a provocation. Leadership, like many things in life, is not a matter of black and white, good or bad. Our purpose has been to invite you, the reader, to pause, to reflect and, hopefully, to open your mind and receive whatever wisdom we have been able to offer, along with any insights which your own musings may have generated. We never intended to write 'the definitive manual' on leadership because there is so much which is situational. It may be correct at certain times to be ambiguous and at other times it might be better to ensure that the 'un' is placed before the 'ambiguous'. Perhaps there we have the ultimate clue to successful leadership: that this book is an attempt to help us to be flexible, to give us choices as to how we act and what we say. We leave you with this final belief: the leader who shows the greatest flexibility in thinking and behaviour *will* have the greatest influence.

Go forth, believe and lead!

THE CODE
BREAKERS

IAN MILLS is CEO of Transform Performance International. He has held leadership roles in the FMCG, financial and technology sectors. Since 1999 he has been a leading light in the building of a globally successful performance-improvement consultancy that has delivered solutions in over 60 countries. From Lima in the west to Beijing in the east, Ian has led behaviour-change and transformation projects with famous-name corporations such as Hewlett-Packard, Deloitte and Maersk.

MARK RIDLEY is a founding Director at Transform Performance International. He has worked as a strategist, chair and facilitator with global brands, investment houses and academic institutions for over 25 years, in 60 countries. Mark's easy manner and ability to ask the tough questions in an engaging way ensure that he is in constant demand. His creativity has ensured that Transform Performance International has a well-earned reputation for inspiring leadership and coaching talent, growing sales and transforming the way people communicate. In short, delivering results through change.

PROFESSOR BEN LAKER is a globally renowned scholar and outstanding university educator who provides academic direction and leadership to research, executive development and education within the subject area of leadership at Henley Business School. His scholarly output appears in world class academic and practitioner journals including *Harvard Business Review* and *The Washington Post*, informs government policy and shapes how thousands of organizations around the world are managed and led. He is retained by the BBC, Bloomberg and Sky News to provide expert commentary on business, economic and political affairs.

ADAM PACIFICO is a barrister and faculty member for Duke Corporate Education. He was previously the education and development group's Managing Director, based in London. Adam has personally trained over 40,000 people globally and worked with a diverse range of clients, from Google, the UK's National Crime Agency and Rolls-Royce to the International Criminal Court. He continues to work with senior leadership teams on large-scale and complex global solutions across disciplines, geographies and talent levels. Adam is a regular keynote speaker and conference chair.

BIBLIOGRAPHY

Akkawi, Yazin. "1 Characteristic Most People Don't Realize
Successful Entrepreneurs Have." *Inc.*, November 29, 2017.
https://www.inc.com/yazin-akkawi/the-one-thing-most-people-dont-
understand-about-becoming-a-successful-entrepreneur.html.

American College of Healthcare Executives, "About CEOs." ACHE, 2019.
https://www.ache.org/learning-center/research/about-ceos.

Aristotle. *The Art of Rhetoric*. Edited by Harvey Yunis. Translated by Robin
Waterfield. Oxford University Press, 2018.

Arkes, Hal R. "A Levels of Processing Interpretation of
Dual-System Theories of Judgment and Decision Making."
Theory & Psychology 26, no. 4 (August 2016): 459–75.
https://doi.org/10.1177/0959354316642878.

Arntz, Arnoud, Michael Rauner, and Marcel Van den Hout.
"'If I Feel Anxious, There Must Be Danger': *Ex-Consequentia*
Reasoning in Inferring Danger in Anxiety Disorders." *Behaviour
Research and Therapy* 33, no. 8 (November 1995): 917–25.
https://doi.org/10.1016/0005-7967(95)00032-S.

Balague, Guillem. *Pep Guardiola: Another Way of Winning: The Biography*.
Orion, 2013.

Banks, Sydney. *The Missing Link: Reflections on Philosophy and Spirit*.
Lone Pine Publishing, 2016.

Bass, Bernard M. "From Transactional to Transformational
Leadership: Learning to Share the Vision." *Organizational
Dynamics* 18, no. 3 (December 1990): 19–31.
https://doi.org/10.1016/0090-2616(90)90061-S.

Blanchard, Ken, John P. Carlos, and Alan Randolph. *Empowerment Takes
More Than a Minute*. Berrett-Koehler Publishers, 2001.

Bonabeau, Eric. "Don't Trust Your Gut." *Harvard Business Review*, May 2003.
https://hbr.org/2003/05/dont-trust-your-gut.

Bonnell, Sunny. "4 Leaders Who Won by Following Their Instincts
(Despite Being Told They Were Crazy)." *Inc.*, January 22, 2018.

Braden, Michelle. "In Leadership, Influence Is Not a Given." *Forbes*, June 2018.

Bradt, George. "How Leaders Influence Contribution And Commitment
While Managers Direct Compliance." *Forbes*, September 2017.

Browning, Geil. "Q&A with Emergenetics Founder
Dr. Geil Browning." Emergenetics International, 2016.
https://www.emergenetics.com/qa-with-emergenetics-founder-
dr-geil-browning/.

Butet-Roch, Laurence. "Pictures Reveal the Isolated Lives of Japan's Social Recluses." *National Geographic*, February 14, 2018.

Carus, Felicity. "Adam Werbach: Lifelong Sustainability Champion." *The Guardian*, May 8, 2012.

Cherniss, Cary, Melissa Extein, Daniel Goleman, and Roger P. Weissberg. "Emotional Intelligence: What Does the Research Really Indicate?" *Educational Psychologist* 41, no. 4 (December 2006): 239–45. https://doi.org/10.1207/s15326985ep4104_4.

Coiné, Ted, and Mark Babbitt. *A World Gone Social: How Companies Must Adapt to Survive*. AMACOM, 2014.

Conger, Jay A., and Rabindra N. Kanungo. "Toward a Behavioral Theory of Charismatic Leadership in Organizational Settings." *Academy of Management Review* 12, no. 4 (October 1987): 637–47. https://doi.org/10.5465/amr.1987.4306715.

Corporate Executive Board, "Companies Not Ready to Realize Promise of Big Data According to Corporate Executive Board." *Cision PR Newswire*, Sept 7, 2011. https://www.prnewswire.com/news-releases/companies-not-ready-to-realize-promise-of-big-data-according-to-corporate-executive-board-129366398.html.

Covey, Stephen R. *7 Habits of Highly Effective People*. Simon & Schuster UK, 2013.

Daisley, Bruce. *The Joy of Work: 30 Ways to Fix Your Work Culture and Fall In Love With Your Job Again*. Random House Business, 2019.

Dapp, Voting. *Shift White Paper*. Duke Corporate Education, 2016, 1–33.

"David Pendleton." Pendleton King, 2019. https://pendletonking.com/david-pendleton/.

Dhaliwal, Gurpreet. "Going with Your Gut." *Journal of General Internal Medicine* 26, no. 2 (February 2011): 107–9. https://doi.org/10.1007/s11606-010-1578-4.

Drehmer, David E., and James E. Bordieri. "Hiring Decisions for Disabled Workers: The Hidden Bias." *Rehabilitation Psychology* 30, no. 3 (1985): 157–64. https://doi.org/10.1037/h0091030.

Elkins, Kathleen. "Jack Dorsey Wakes up at 5 a.m. and Walks 5 Miles to Work – Here's What Happened When I Tried That Routine for a Week." *CNBC*, February 19, 2019. https://www.cnbc.com/2019/02/15/i-tried-twitter-ceo-jack-dorseys-early-morning-routine-for-a-week.html.

European Commission, "One Trillion Euro to Invest in Europe's Future – the EU's Budget Framework 2014-2020," European Commission press release, November 19, 2013. http://europa.eu/rapid/press-release_IP-13-1096_en.htm.

Fancisco, Janice and Cynthia Burnett. "Deliberate Intuition: Giving Intuitive Insights Their Rightful Place in the Creative Problem Solving Thinking Skills Model." *Creativity and Innovation Management*, 3 (2010): 236–53.

Fridman, Adam. "Rethinking What Makes Thought Leadership Great." *Inc.*, Feb 2, 2016. https://www.inc.com/adam-fridman/rethinking-what-makes-thought-leadership-great.html.

Frogner, Bianca K. "Update on the Stock and Supply of Health Services Researchers in the United States." *Health Services Research* 53 (October 2018): 3945–66. https://doi.org/10.1111/1475-6773.12988.

Fry, Richard. "Millennials Are Largest Generation in the U.S. Labor Force." Fact Tank, Pew Research Center, April 11, 2018. https://www.pewresearch.org/fact-tank/2018/04/11/millennials-largest-generation-us-labor-force/.

Gelatt, H. B. "Positive Uncertainty: A New Decision-Making Framework for Counseling." *Journal of Counseling Psychology* 36, no. 2 (April, 1989): 252–56. https://doi.org/10.1037/0022-0167.36.2.252.

Gerdes, Eugenia Proctor, and Douglas M. Garber. "Sex Bias in Hiring: Effects of Job Demands and Applicant Competence." *Sex Roles* 9, no. 3 (March 1983): 307–19. https://doi.org/10.1007/BF00289666.

Ghemawat, Pankaj. "Evolving Ideas about Business Strategy." *Business History Review* 90, no. 04 (December, 2016): 727–49. https://doi.org/10.1017/S0007680516000702.

Ghemawat, Pankaj. *The New Global Road Map: Enduring Strategies for Turbulent Times*. Massachusetts: Harvard Business Review Press, 2018.

Goleman, Daniel. "Leadership That Gets Results." *Harvard Business Review* 78, no. 2 (2000): 78–90. http://www.powerelectronics.ac.uk/documents/leadership-that-gets-results.pdf.

Goodall, Amanda H. "Physician-Leaders and Hospital Performance: Is There an Association?" *Social Science & Medicine* 73, no. 4 (August, 2011): 535–39. https://doi.org/10.1016/J.SOCSCIMED.2011.06.025.

Greyser, Stephen A, and Mats Urde. "What Does Your Corporate Brand Stand For?" *Harvard Business Review*, Jan-Feb 2019. https://hbr.org/2019/01/what-does-your-corporate-brand-stand-for.

Groysberg, Boris, and Michael Slind. *Talk, Inc. How Trusted Leaders Use Conversation to Power Their Organizations*. Harvard Business Review Press, 2012.

"Guide: Understand Team Effectiveness." re: Work, n.d.

Hamel, Gary, and Polly LaBarre. "How to Lead When You're Not in Charge." *Harvard Business Review*, May 2013. https://hbr.org/2013/05/how-to-lead-when-youre-not-in.

Harvard Business Review, "When Hiring Execs, Context Matters Most." *Harvard Business Review*, 2017, https://hbr.org/2017/09/when-hiring-execs-context-matters-most.

Hern, Alex. "Tim Berners-Lee on 30 years of the world wide web: 'We can get the web we want.'" *The Guardian*, March 12, 2019: 1–4. https://www.theguardian.com/technology/2019/mar/12/tim-berners-lee-on-30-years-of-the-web-if-we-dream-a-little-we-can-get-the-web-we-want.

Heskett, James L., Thomas O. Jones, Gary W. Loveman, W. Earl Sesser Jr, and Leonard A. Schlesinger. "Putting the Service-Profit Chain to Work." *Harvard Business Review*, July-August 2008. https://hbr.org/2008/07/putting-the-service-profit-chain-to-work.

Hiatt, Brian. "Twitter CEO Jack Dorsey: The Rolling Stone Interview." *Rolling Stone*, January 23, 2019.

Highhouse, Scott. "Stubborn Reliance on Intuition and Subjectivity in Employee Selection." *Industrial and Organizational Psychology* 1, no. 3 (September 2008): 333–42. https://doi.org/10.1111/j.1754-9434.2008.00058.x.

Hill, Linda, and Kent Lineback. "If You Don't Want To Influence Others, You Can't Lead." *Harvard Business Review*, February 2011. https://hbr.org/2011/02/if-you-dont-want-to-influence.html.

"If You Can't Keep Your Spreadsheets Straight, Here's the Simple Solution," 2018. https://www.inc.com/intel/spreadsheet-overload-heres-how-to-know-its-time-to-move-to-software.html?cid=hmsub3.

Inglehart, Ronald F. *Cultural Evolution: People's Motivations Are Changing, and Reshaping the World*. Cambridge University Press, 2018.

Isaac, Carol, Barbara Lee, and Molly Carnes. "Interventions That Affect Gender Bias in Hiring: A Systematic Review." *Academic Medicine: Journal of the Association of American Medical Colleges* 84, no. 10 (October 2009): 1440–46. https://doi.org/10.1097/ACM.0b013e3181b6ba00.

Kahneman, Daniel. *Thinking, Fast and Slow*. Penguin, 2012.

Keller Johnson, Lauren. "Exerting Influence Without Authority." *Harvard Business Review*, February 2008. https://hbr.org/2008/02/exerting-influence-without-aut.

Key, Mary Ritchie. *Paralanguage and Kinesics (Nonverbal Communication)*. Scarecrow Press, Inc., 1975. https://eric.ed.gov/?id=ED143053.

Klayman, Joshua, Jack B. Soll, Claudia González-Vallejo, and Sema Barlas. "Overconfidence: It Depends on How, What, and Whom You Ask." *Organizational Behavior and Human Decision Processes* 79, no. 3 (September 1999): 216–47. https://doi.org/10.1006/OBHD.1999.2847.

Kramer, Garret. *The Path of No Resistance: Why Overcoming Is Simpler than You Think*. Greenleaf Book Group LLC, 2015.

Kutschera, Ida, and Mike H. Ryan. "Implications of Intuition for Strategic Thinking: Practical Recommendations for Gut Thinkers." *S.A.M. Advanced Management Journal* 74, no. 3 (2009). https://search.proquest.com/openview/3b46749157f93df1fef4fc8fded a654d/1?pq-origsite=gscholar&cbl=40946.

"Leading Ideas: Look for Excellence in Others." Fast Company, 2005. https://www.fastcompany.com/672502/leading-ideas-look-excellence-others.

Lerner, Michael P. "Stress at the Workplace." *Issues in Radical Therapy* 10, no. 3 (1982): 14–16.

Lunenburg, Fred C. "Leadership versus Management: A Key Distinction – At Least in Theory." *International Journal of Management, Business and Administration* 14, no. 1 (2011). https://cs.anu.edu.au/courses/comp3120/local_docs/readings/ Lunenburg_LeadershipVersusManagement.pdf.

MacGregor Burns, James. *Transformational Leadership: The Pursuit of Happiness*. Grove/Atlantic, 2003.

Mackay, Justin. "Employee Engagement Survey Overview." Primary Colour Surveys, 2014. https://www.edgecumbe.co.uk/engagement-surveys/.

Matthews, Derek. "Are You A Transactional Or Transformational Leader?" *Forbes* (November 2018).

McLeod, Saul. "The Interview Method." Simply Psychology, 2014. https://www.simplypsychology.org/interviews.html.

Meeker, Mary. Internet Trends 2018. Kleiner Perkins, 2018, 294. https://kleinerperkins.com/perspectives/internet-trends-report-2018.

Mellon, Liz. "Ditch the Wonder Woman Complex. Resilience Is What You Need." *Dialogue Review*, June 13, 2016.

Mental Health Foundation. "Stressed Nation: 74% of UK 'overwhelmed or unable to cope' at some point in the past year," Mental Health Foundation, press release, May 14, 2018. https://www.mentalhealth.org.uk/news/stressed-nation-74-uk-overwhelmed-or-unable-cope-some-point-past-year.

Milczarek, Malgorzata, Elke Schneider, and Eusebio Rial González (European Agency for Safety and Health at Work). *European Risk Observatory Report, OSH in figures: stress at work – facts and figures*. European Communities, 2009. http://bookshop.europa.eu.

Miller, C. Chet, and R. Duane Ireland. "Intuition in Strategic Decision Making: Friend or Foe in the Fast-Paced 21st Century?" *Academy of Management Perspectives* 19, no. 1 (February 2005): 19–30. https://doi.org/10.5465/ame.2005.15841948.

Mills, Ian, Mark Ridley, Ben Laker, and Tim Chapman. *The Salesperson's Secret Code: The Belief Systems That Distinguish Winners.* LID Publishing, 2017. http://lidpublishing.com/book/salesperson-secret-code/.

Mtumbuka, Matthews. "The 40-70 Colin Powell Rule." *The Nation,* February 12, 2015. https://mwnation.com/40-70-colin-powell-rule/.

Neckerman, Kathryn M., and Joleen Kirschenman. "Hiring Strategies, Racial Bias, and Inner-City Workers." *Social Problems* 38, no. 4 (November 1991): 433–47. https://doi.org/10.2307/800563.

Nielsen, Liesl. "Oprah Tells Utah Audience That 'Your Legacy Is Every Life You Touch.'" KSL.com, 2019. https://www.ksl.com/article/46506476/oprah-tells-utah-audience-that-your-legacy-is-every-life-you-touch.

Nilsson, Jeff. "Why Did Henry Ford Double His Minimum Wage?" *The Saturday Evening Post,* January 3, 2014.

Nisbett, Richard E., and Timothy D. Wilson. "The Halo Effect: Evidence for Unconscious Alteration of Judgments." *Journal of Personality and Social Psychology* 35, no. 4 (1977): 250–56. https://doi.org/10.1037/0022-3514.35.4.250.

Norm, "How To Fix Overthinking." *Striving Strategically*, 2019.

Novak, Jamie. *The Get Organized Answer Book.* Sourcebooks, Inc, 2009.

Novet, Jordan. "Uber CEO Firm on Surge Pricing, Regardless of the Consequences." *Venture Beat,* January 8, 2014. https://venturebeat.com/2014/01/08/uber-ceo-firm-on-surge-pricing-regardless-of-the-consequences/.

Parr, Sam. "Jack Dorsey Wakes Up Every Morning at 5:00 AM." *The Hustle,* December 22, 2015.

Pascale, Richard T., Mark Millemann, and Linda Gioja. *Surfing the Edge of Chaos: The Laws of Nature and the New Laws of Business.* Three Rivers Press, 2000. https://books.google.com/books?id=lhahvT41XkEC&pgis=1.

Patton, John R. "Intuition in Decisions." *Management Decision* 41, no. 10 (December 2003): 989–96. https://doi.org/10.1108/00251740310509517.

Pendleton, David, and Adrian Furnham. *Leadership: All You Need to Know. Leadership: All You Need to Know.* Palgrave Macmillan, 2011. https://doi.org/10.1057/9780230354425.

Pink, Daniel. *Drive: The Surprising Truth about What Motivates Us*. Canongate Books Ltd, 2011.

Productivityist. "3 Ways to Power Through Your Email Inbox." https://productivityist.com/emptyyouremailinbox/.

Rath, Tom, and Gallup Press. *Strengths Based Leadership: Great Leaders, Teams, and Why People Follow*. Gallup Press, 2016.

Ray, Michael, and Rochelle Myers. "Practical Intuition." In *Intuition in Organisations*, edited by Weston H. Agor, 247–62. Sage Publications, 1990.

Richerson, Peter J., and Robert Boyd. "The Evolution of Subjective Commitment to Groups: A Tribal Instincts Hypothesis." In *The Evolution of Subjective Commitment*, edited by R.M. Nesse. Russell Sage Foundation, 2001. http://www.des.ucdavis.edu/faculty/Richerson/comgrps.pdf.

Rosenbaum, Ron. *Explaining Hitler*. Da Capo Press, 1998.

Rozovsky, Julia. "The Five Keys to a Successful Google Team." re: Work, 2015.

Sankar, Carol. "The Most Successful Leaders Make These 4 Boundaries Clear." *Inc.*, June 28, 2018. https://www.inc.com/carol-sankar/4-boundaries-you-must-implement-today-to-become-a-successful-leader.html.

Schlottman, Andrea. "Samuel Beckett: Fail Better and 'Worstward Ho!'" *Books on the Wall*, 2019. https://booksonthewall.com/blog/samuel-beckett-quote-fail-better/.

Schwantes, Marcel. "Bill Gates, Steve Jobs, and Warren Buffett All Agree: These 3 Hiring Strategies Will Land You the Best People." *Inc.*, February 11, 2019. https://www.inc.com/marcel-schwantes/bill-gates-steve-jobs-agree-these-2-brilliant-hiring-strategies-will-land-you-best-people.html.

Schwarzkopf, Norman. *It Doesn't Take a Hero: The Autobiography of General H. Norman Schwarzkopf*. Bantam, 1993.

Searle, Maddy. "Conan Doyle: What Was the Inspiration for Sherlock Holmes?" *The Scotsman*, January 23, 2017. https://www.scotsman.com/200voices/literary-titans/conan-doyle-sherlock-holmes-author/.

Sethi, Ramit. "How to Deal With Difficult Coworkers (Proven Tips & Strategies)." I Will Teach You to be Rich (blog), June 10, 2019. https://www.iwillteachyoutoberich.com/blog/be-the-expert-how-would-you-respond-to-this-co-worker/.

Siegrist, Johannes. "Stress at Work." In *International Encyclopedia of the Social & Behavioral Sciences: Second Edition*, Editor-in-Chief James D. Wright, 546–50. Elsevier, 2015. https://doi.org/10.1016/B978-0-08-097086-8.73023-6.

Spaulding, Dave. "Intuitive Decisionmaking." *Police: The Law Enforcement Magazine* 29, no. 3 (March 2005): 62–64. https://www.ncjrs.gov/App/AbstractDB/AbstractDBDetails. aspx?id=209428.

Stoller, Kristin. "Global 2000: The World's Largest Public Companies 2018." *Forbes*, June 2018. https://www.forbes.com/sites/kristinstoller/2018/06/06/the-worlds-largest-public-companies-2018/#2ad0cf69769f.

Strategy&. *What drives a company's success? Highlights of survey findings*. PwC, 2013. https://www.strategyand-what-drives-a-companys-success.pdf.

Duke Corporate Education. *What's Next in Leadership: New Mindsets, New Behaviours, New Potential*. Duke Corporate Education, 2018.

Tabaka, Marla. "Steve Jobs & You Have This in Common." *Inc.*, July 30, 2012. https://www.inc.com/marla-tabaka/steve-jobs-intuition-you-have-this-in-common.html.

Trammell, Joel. "5 Responsibilities of a CEO: Make Good Decisions." The American CEO, 2013. https://theamericanceo.com/2013/07/02/5-responsibilities-of-a-ceo-make-good-decisions/.

Travis, Toogood, Spadorcia Sarah, Mishra Bharat, and Mishra Jitendra. "How to Manage Difficult Employees." *Advances in Management* 10, no. 1 (January 2017): 1–6. https://www.questia.com/library/journal/1P3-4294250371/how-to-manage-difficult-employees.

Tsipursky, Gleb. "Autopilot vs. Intentional System: The Rider and the Elephant." Intentional Insights, 2014. https://intentionalinsights.org/autopilot-vs-intentional-system-the-rider-and-the-elephant/.

Tsipursky, Gleb. "Protect Your Relationships by Cutting Off Your Anchors." Intentional Insights, 2015. https://intentionalinsights.org/protect-your-relationships-by-cutting-off-your-anchors/.

Tversky, Amos, and Daniel Kahneman. "Judgment under Uncertainty: Heuristics and Biases." In *Utility, Probability, and Human Decision Making*, edited by D. Wendt and C. Vlek, 141–62. Springer Netherlands, 1975. https://doi.org/10.1007/978-94-010-1834-0_8.

U.S. News. "Best Hospitals by Specialty: National Rankings." *U.S. News*, July 29, 2019. https://health.usnews.com/best-hospitals/rankings.

Vardy, Mike. *The Productivityist Playbook*. Productivityist, 2016.

Vielmetter, Georg, and Yvonne Sell. *Leadership 2030: The Six Megatrends You Need to Understand to Lead Your Company into the Future*. AMACOM, 2014.

Vize, Richard. "Why Doctors Don't Dare Go into Management." *The BMJ*, February 2015. https://www.bmj.com/bmj/section-pdf/891755?path=/bmj/350/7997/Feature.full.pdf.

Walker, Ben. "Justin Ferrell Is the Essential Voice for Design-Thinking in Organizations." *Dialogue Review*, September 25, 2019.

Wasserman, Noam, Nitin Nohria, and Bharat Anand. "When Does Leadership Matter? A Contingent Opportunities View of CEO Leadership." In *Handbook of Leadership Theory and Practice*, edited by Nitin Nohria and Rakesh Khurana , Chapter 2. Harvard Business Press, 2010. https://www.hbs.edu/faculty/Pages/item.aspx?num=37549.

Weber, Max, and Keith Tribe. *Economy and Society*. Harvard University Press, 2019.

Weinman, Mitzi. *It's About Time! Transforming Chaos into Calm, A to Z*. iUniverse, 2014.

Williams, Andrew. "6 Ways Hesitant Leaders Can Embrace Social Media." *Business News Daily*, July 20, 2017.

Zielenziger, Michael. *Shutting Out The Sun: How Japan Created Its Own Lost Generation*. Ballantine Books Inc., 2007.

ENDNOTES

1. Ian Mills et al., *The Salesperson's Secret Code: The Belief Systems That Distinguish Winners* (LID Publishing, 2017), http://lidpublishing.com/book/sales-person-secret-code/.

2. Mills et al.

3. Mills et al.

4. Mary Meeker, Internet Trends 2018 (Kleiner Perkins, 2018), https://www.kleinerperkins.com/perspectives/internet-trends-report-2018.

5. Kristin Stoller, "Global 2000: The World's Largest Public Companies 2018," *Forbes*, June 2018, https://www.forbes.com/sites/kristinstoller/2018/06/06/the-worlds-largest-public-companies-2018/#2ad0cf69769f.

6. Richard T. Pascale, Mark Millemann, and Linda Gioja, *Surfing the Edge of Chaos: The Laws of Nature and the New Laws of Business*, (Three Rivers Press, 2000), https://books.google.com/books?id=lhahvT41XkEC&pgis=1.

7. Pankaj Ghemawat, *The New Global RoadMap: Enduring Strategies for Turbulent Times* (Harvard Business Review Press, 2018).

8. Pankaj Ghemawat, "Evolving Ideas about Business Strategy," *Business History Review* 90, no. 4 (December 2016): 727–49, https://doi.org/10.1017/S0007680516000702.

9. David Pendleton and Adrian Furnham, *Leadership: All You Need to Know* (Palgrave Macmillan, 2011), https://doi.org/10.1057/9780230354425.

10. Pendleton and Furnham.

11. Noam Wasserman, Nitin Nohria, and Bharat Anand, "When Does Leadership Matter? A Contingent Opportunities View of CEO Leadership," in *Handbook of Leadership Theory and Practice*, ed. Nitin Nohria and Rakesh Khurana (Harvard Business Press, 2010), Chap. 2, https://www.hbs.edu/faculty/Pages/item.aspx?num=37549.

12. Ian Mills et al., *The Salesperson's Secret Code: The Belief Systems That Distinguish Winners* (LID Publishing, 2017), http://lidpublishing.com/book/sales-person-secret-code/.

13. Bruce Daisley, *The Joy of Work: 30 Ways to Fix Your Work Culture and Fall In Love With Your Job Again* (Random House Business, 2019).

14. Norman Schwarzkopf, *It Doesn't Take a Hero: The Autobiography of General H. Norman Schwarzkopf* (Bantam, 1993).

15. Richard Vize, "Why Doctors Don't Dare Go into Management," *The BMJ* (February 2015), https://www.bmj.com/bmj/section-pdf/891755?path=/bmj/350/7997/Feature.full.pdf.

16. Amanda H. Goodall, "Physician-Leaders and Hospital Performance: Is There an Association?," *Social Science & Medicine* 73, no. 4 (August 2011): 535–39, https://doi.org/10.1016/J.SOCSCIMED.2011.06.025.

17. Bianca K. Frogner, "Update on the Stock and Supply of Health Services Researchers in the United States," *Health Services Research* 53 (October 2018): 3945–66, https://doi.org/10.1111/1475-6773.12988.

18. Vize, "Why Doctors Don't Dare Go into Management."

19. American College of Healthcare Executives, "About CEOs," ACHE, 2019, https://www.ache.org/learning-center/research/about-ceos.

20. Corboz, Anne-Valeria, Davis, John, and Patel, Vishal. *Is Your Organization Ready To Shift?* (Duke Corporate Education, 2019). https://www.dukece.com/insights/is-your-organization-ready-to-shift/.

21. Duke Corporate Education, *What's Next in Leadership: New Mindsets, New Behaviours, New Potential*, (Duke Corporate Education, 2018).

22. Daniel Goleman, "Leadership That Gets Results.," *Harvard Business Review* (March-April 2000), http://hbr.org/2000/03/leadership-that-gets-results.

23. Johannes Siegrist, "Stress at Work." In *International Encyclopediaof the Social & Behavioral Sciences: Second Edition*, Editor-in-Chief James D. Wright, Elsevier, 2015. https://doi.org/10.1016/B978-0-08-097086-8.73023-6.

24. Ramit Sethi, "How to Deal With Difficult Coworkers (Proven Tips & Strategies)," I Will Teach You to be Rich (blog), June 10, 2019, https://www.iwillteachyoutoberich.com/blog/be-the-expert-how-would-you-respond-to-this-co-worker/.

25. Malgorzata Milczarek, Elke Schneider, and Eusebio Rial González (European Agency for Safety and Health at Work), *European Risk Observatory Report, OSH in figures: stress at work – facts and figures* (European Communities, 2009), http://bookshop.europa.eu.

26. European Commission, "One Trillion Euro to Invest in Europe's Future – the EU's Budget Framework 2014-2020," European Commission press release, November 19, 2013, http://europa.eu/rapid/press-release_IP-13-1096_en.htm.

27. Mental Health Foundation, "Stressed Nation: 74% of UK 'overwhelmed or unable to cope' at some point in the past year," Mental Health Foundation press release, May 14, 2018, https://www.mentalhealth.org.uk/news/stressed-nation-74-uk-overwhelmed-or-unable-cope-some-point-past-year.

28. Michael P. Lerner, "Stress at the Workplace," *Issues in Radical Therapy* 10, no. 3 (1982): 14–16.

29. Garret Kramer, *The Path of No Resistance: Why Overcoming Is Simpler than You Think* (Greenleaf Book Group LLC, 2015).

30. Sydney Banks, *The Missing Link: Reflections on Philosophy and Spirit* (Lone Pine Publishing, 2016).

31. Rachel Dresdale, "6 Tips On Working Smarter, Not Harder This Year," *Forbes*, December 2016. https://www.forbes.com/sites/rachelritlop/2016/12/28/6-tips-on-working-smart-not-hard-this-year/#23fdfddb29f5.

32. Jamie Novak, *The Get Organized Answer Book* (Sourcebooks, Inc, 2009).

33. Mitzi Weinman, *It's About Time! Transforming Chaos into Calm, A to Z* (iUniverse, 2014).

34. Mike Vardy, *The Productivityist Playbook* (Productivityist, 2016).

35. Productivityist. "3 Ways to Power Through Your Email Inbox." https://productivityist.com/emptyyouremailinbox/.

36. Liz Mellon, "Ditch the Wonder Woman Complex. Resilience Is What You Need," *Dialogue Review*, June 13, 2016.

37. Guillem Balague, *Pep Guardiola: Another Way of Winning: The Biography* (Orion, 2013).

38. Michelle Braden, "In Leadership, Influence Is Not a Given," *Forbes*, June 2018.

39. Alex Hern, "Tim Berners-Lee on 30 years of the world wide web: 'We can get the web we want,'" *The Guardian*, March 12, 2019: 1–4, https://www.theguardian.com/technology/2019/mar/12/tim-berners-lee-on-30-years-of-the-web-if-we-dream-a-little-we-can-get-the-web-we-want.

40. Max Weber and Keith Tribe, *Economy and Society* (Harvard University Press, 2019).

41. Derek Matthews, "Are You A Transactional Or Transformational Leader?," *Forbes* (November 2018).

42. James MacGregor Burns, *Transformational Leadership: The Pursuit of Happiness* (Grove/Atlantic, 2003).

43. Paul Allen, *Idea Man*, (Penguin Press, 2011).

44. Gary Hamel and Polly LaBarre, "How to Lead When You're Not in Charge," *Harvard Business Review*, May 2013, https://hbr.org/2013/05/how-to-lead-when-youre-not-in.

45. Lauren Keller Johnson, "Exerting Influence Without Authority," *Harvard Business Review*, February 2008, https://hbr.org/2008/02/exerting-influence-without-aut.

46. Linda Hill and Kent Lineback, "If You Don't Want To Influence Others, You Can't Lead," *Harvard Business Review*, February 2011, https://hbr.org/2011/02/if-you-dont-want-to-influence.html.

47. Bernard M. Bass, "From Transactional to Transformational Leadership: Learning to Share the Vision," *Organizational Dynamics* 18, no. 3 (December 1990): 19–31, https://doi.org/10.1016/0090-2616(90)90061-S.

48. Richard Fry, "Millennials Are Largest Generation in the U.S. Labor Force," Fact Tank, Pew Research Center, April 11, 2018, https://www.pewresearch.org/fact-tank/2018/04/11/millennials-largest-generation-us-labor-force/.

49. Ted Coiné and Mark Babbitt, *A World Gone Social: How Companies Must Adapt to Survive* (AMACOM, 2014).

50. Stephen A. Greyser and Mats Urde, "What Does Your Corporate Brand Stand For?," *Harvard Business Review*, Jan-Feb 2019, https://hbr.org/2019/01/what-does-your-corporate-brand-stand-for.

51. Andrew Williams, "6 Ways Hesitant Leaders Can Embrace Social Media," *Business News Daily*, July 20, 2017.

52. Adam Fridman, "Rethinking What Makes Thought Leadership Great," *Inc.*, Feb 2, 2016, https://www.inc.com/adam-fridman/rethinking-what-makes-thought-leadership-great.html.

53. Stephen R. Covey, *7 Habits of Highly Effective People* (Simon & Schuster UK, 2013).

54. George Bradt, "How Leaders Influence Contribution And Commitment While Managers Direct Compliance," *Forbes*, September 2017.

55. Aristotle, *The Art of Rhetoric*, ed. Harvey Yunis, trans. Robin Waterfield (Oxford University Press, 2018).

56. Boris Groysberg and Michael Slind, *Talk, Inc. How Trusted Leaders Use Conversation to Power Their Organizations* (Harvard Business Review Press, 2012).

57. Geil Browning, "Q&A with Emergenetics Founder Dr. Geil Browning," Emergenetics International, 2016, https://www.emergenetics.com/qa-with-emergenetics-founder-dr-geil-browning/.

58. Cary Cherniss et al., "Emotional Intelligence: What Does the Research Really Indicate?," *Educational Psychologist* 41, no. 4 (December 2006): 239–45, https://doi.org/10.1207/s15326985ep4104_4.

59. Eric Bonabeau, "Don't Trust Your Gut," *Harvard Business Review*, May 2003, https://hbr.org/2003/05/dont-trust-your-gut.

60. Corporate Executive Board, "Companies Not Ready to Realize Promise of Big Data According to Corporate Executive Board," *Cision PR Newswire*, Sept 7, 2011, https://www.prnewswire.com/news-releases/companies-not-ready-to-realize-promise-of-big-data-according-to-corporate-executive-board-129366398.html.

61. Janice Fancisco and Cynthia Burnett, "Deliberate Intuition: Giving Intuitive Insights Their Rightful Place in the Creative Problem Solving Thinking Skills Model," *Creativity and Innovation Management* 3 (2010): 236–53.

62. Ida Kutschera and Mike H. Ryan, "Implications of Intuition for Strategic Thinking: Practical Recommendations for Gut Thinkers," *S.A.M. Advanced Management Journal* 74, no. 3 (2009), https://search.proquest.com/openview/3b46749157f93df1fef4fc8fdeda654d/1?pq-origsite=gscholar&cbl=40946.

63. Matthews Mtumbuka, "The 40-70 Colin Powell Rule," *The Nation*, February 12, 2015, https://mwnation.com/40-70-colin-powell-rule/.

64. Norm, "How To Fix Overthinking," *Striving Strategically*, 2019.

65. Joel Trammell, "5 Responsibilities of a CEO: Make Good Decisions," The American CEO, 2013, https://theamericanceo.com/2013/07/02/5-responsibilities-of-a-ceo-make-good-decisions/.

66. John R. Patton, "Intuition in Decisions," *Management Decision* 41, no. 10 (December 2003): 989–96, https://doi.org/10.1108/00251740310509517.

67. Gurpreet Dhaliwal, "Going with Your Gut," *Journal of General Internal Medicine* 26, no. 2 (February 2011): 107–9, https://doi.org/10.1007/s11606-010-1578-4.

68. H. B. Gelatt, "Positive Uncertainty: A New Decision-Making Framework for Counseling," *Journal of Counseling Psychology* 36, no. 2 (April 1989): 252–56, https://doi.org/10.1037/0022-0167.36.2.252.

69. Peter J. Richerson and Robert Boyd, "The Evolution of Subjective Commitment to Groups: A Tribal Instincts Hypothesis," in *The Evolution of Subjective Commitment*, ed. R.M. Nesse (Russell Sage Foundation, 2001), http://www.des.ucdavis.edu/faculty/Richerson/comgrps.pdf.

70. Mary Ritchie Key, *Paralanguage and Kinesics (Nonverbal Communication)* (Scarecrow Press, Inc., 1975), https://eric.ed.gov/?id=ED143053.

71. Gleb Tsipursky, "Autopilot vs. Intentional System: The Rider and the Elephant," Intentional Insights, 2014, https://intentionalinsights.org/autopilot-vs-intentional-system-the-rider-and-the-elephant/.

72. Amos Tversky and Daniel Kahneman, "Judgment under Uncertainty: Heuristics and Biases," in Utility, Probability, and Human Decision Making, ed. D. Wendt and C. Vlek (Springer Netherlands, 1975), 141–62, https://doi.org/10.1007/978-94-010-1834-0_8.

73. Daniel Kahneman, *Thinking, Fast and Slow* (Penguin, 2012).

74. Hal R. Arkes, "A Levels of Processing Interpretation of Dual-System Theories of Judgment and Decision Making," *Theory & Psychology* 26, no. 4 (August 2016): 459–75, https://doi.org/10.1177/0959354316642878.

75. Richard E. Nisbett and Timothy D. Wilson, "The Halo Effect: Evidence for Unconscious Alteration of Judgments," *Journal of Personality and Social Psychology* 35, no. 4 (1977): 250–56, https://doi.org/10.1037/0022-3514.35.4.250.

76. Dave Spaulding, "Intuitive Decisionmaking," *Police: The Law Enforcement Magazine* 29, no. 3 (March 2005): 62–64, https://www.ncjrs.gov/App/AbstractDB/AbstractDBDetails.aspx?id=209428.

77. C. Chet Miller and R. Duane Ireland, "Intuition in Strategic DecisionMaking: Friend or Foe in the Fast-Paced 21st Century?," *Academy of Management Perspectives* 19, no. 1 (February 2005): 19–30, https://doi.org/10.5465/ame.2005.15841948.

78. Kathryn M. Neckerman and Joleen Kirschenman, "Hiring Strategies, Racial Bias, and Inner-City Workers," *Social Problems* 38, no. 4 (November 1991): 433–47, https://doi.org/10.2307/800563.

79. David E. Drehmer and James E. Bordieri, "Hiring Decisions for Disabled Workers: The Hidden Bias.," *Rehabilitation Psychology* 30, no. 3 (1985): 157–64, https://doi.org/10.1037/h0091030.

80. Eugenia Proctor Gerdes and Douglas M. Garber, "Sex Bias in Hiring: Effects of Job Demands and Applicant Competence," *Sex Roles* 9, no. 3 (March 1983): 307–19, https://doi.org/10.1007/BF00289666.

81. Carol Isaac, Barbara Lee, and Molly Carnes, "Interventions That Affect Gender Bias in Hiring: A Systematic Review," *Academic Medicine: Journal of the Association of American Medical Colleges* 84, no. 10 (October 2009): 1440–46, https://doi.org/10.1097/ACM.0b013e3181b6ba00.

82. Scott Highhouse, "Stubborn Reliance on Intuition and Subjectivity in Employee Selection," *Industrial and Organizational Psychology* 1, no. 03 (September 2008): 333–42, https://doi.org/10.1111/j.1754-9434.2008.00058.x.

83. Joshua Klayman et al., "Overconfidence: It Depends on How, What, and Whom You Ask," *Organizational Behavior and Human Decision Processes* 79, no. 3 (September 1999): 216–47, https://doi.org/10.1006/OBHD.1999.2847.

84. Gleb Tsipursky, "Protect Your Relationships by Cutting Off Your Anchors," Intentional Insights, 2015, https://intentionalinsights.org/protect-your-relationships-by-cutting-off-your-anchors/.

85. Saul McLeod, "The Interview Method," Simply Psychology, 2014, https://www.simplypsychology.org/interviews.html.

86. Arnoud Arntz, Michael Rauner, and Marcel Van den Hout, "'If I Feel Anxious, There Must Be Danger': *Ex-Consequentia* Reasoning in Inferring Danger in Anxiety Disorders," *Behaviour Research and Therapy* 33, no. 8 (November 1995): 917–25, https://doi.org/10.1016/0005-7967(95)00032-S.

87. Michael Ray and Rochelle Myers, "Practical Intuition," in *Intuition in Organizations*, ed. Weston H. Agor (Sage Publications, 1990), 247–62.

88. Maddy Searle, "Conan Doyle: What Was the Inspiration for Sherlock Holmes?," *The Scotsman*, January 23, 2017 https://www.scotsman.com/200voices/literary-titans/conan-doyle-sherlock-holmes-author/.

89. James L. Heskett et al., "Putting the Service-Profit Chain to Work," *Harvard Business Review*, July-August 2008, https://hbr.org/2008/07/putting-the-service-profit-chain-to-work.

90. Jay A. Conger and Rabindra N. Kanungo, "Toward a Behavioral Theory of Charismatic Leadership in Organizational Settings," *Academy of Management Review* 12, no. 4 (October 1987): 637–47, https://doi.org/10.5465/amr.1987.4306715.

91. Dhaliwal, Gurpreet, "Going with Your Gut." J Gen Intern Med 26, No. 2 (November 2010). 107-109.

92. Marla Tabaka, "Steve Jobs & You Have This in Common," *Inc.*, July 30, 2012, https://www.inc.com/marla-tabaka/steve-jobs-intuition-you-have-this-in-common.html.

93. Yazin Akkawi, "1 Characteristic Most People Don't Realize Successful Entrepreneurs Have," *Inc.*, November 29, 2017, https://www.inc.com/yazin-akkawi/the-one-thing-most-people-dont-understand-about-becoming-a-successful-entrepreneur.html.

94. Marla Tabaka, "Steve Jobs & You Have This in Common." *Inc.*, 2012.

95. Felicity Carus, "Adam Werbach: Lifelong Sustainability Champion," *The Guardian*, May 8, 2012.

96. Jeff Nilsson, "Why Did Henry Ford Double His Minimum Wage?," *The Saturday Evening Post*, January 3, 2014.

97. Sunny Bonnell, "4 Leaders Who Won by Following Their Instincts (Despite Being Told They Were Crazy)," *Inc.*, January 22, 2018.

98. Jordan Novet, "Uber CEO Firm on Surge Pricing, Regardless of the Consequences," *Venture Beat*, January 8, 2014, https://venturebeat.com/2014/01/08/uber-ceo-firm-on-surge-pricing-regardless-of-the-consequences/.

99. Ron Rosenbaum, *Explaining Hitler* (Da Capo Press, 1998).

100. Ken Blanchard, John P. Carlos, and Alan Randolph, *Empowerment Takes More Than a Minute* (Berrett-Koehler Publishers, 2001).

101. "David Pendleton," Pendleton King, 2019, https://pendletonking.com/david-pendleton/.

102. Ben Walker, "Justin Ferrell Is the Essential Voice for Design-Thinking in Organizations," *Dialogue Review*, September 25, 2019.

103. Andrea Schlottman, "Samuel Beckett: Fail Better and 'Worstward Ho!,'" Books on the Wall, 2019, https://booksonthewall.com/blog/samuel-beckett-quote-fail-better/.

104. Julia Rozovsky, "The Five Keys to a Successful Google Team," re: Work, 2015.

105. U.S. News, "Best Hospitals by Specialty: National Rankings," *U.S. News*, July 29, 2019, https://health.usnews.com/best-hospitals/rankings.

106. re: Work, "Guide: Understand Team Effectiveness," re: Work, n.d.

107. Carol Sankar, "The Most Successful Leaders Make These 4 Boundaries Clear," *Inc.*, June 28, 2018, https://www.inc.com/carol-sankar/4-boundaries-you-must-implement-today-to-become-a-successful-leader.html.

108. Kathleen Elkins, "Jack Dorsey Wakes up at 5 a.m. and Walks 5 Miles to Work – Here's What Happened When I Tried That Routine for a Week," *CNBC*, February 19, 2019, https://www.cnbc.com/2019/02/15/i-tried-twitter-ceo-jack-dorseys-early-morning-routine-for-a-week.html.

109. Carol Sankar, "The Most Successful Leaders Make These 4 Boundaries Clear." *Inc.*, June 28, 2018, https://www.inc.com/carol-sankar/4-boundaries-you-must-implement-today-to-become-a-successful-leader.html.

110. Brian Hiatt, "Twitter CEO Jack Dorsey: The Rolling Stone Interview," *Rolling Stone*, January 23, 2019.

111. Sam Parr, "Jack Dorsey Wakes Up Every Morning at 5:00 AM," *The Hustle*, December 22, 2015.

112. Sam Parr, "Jack Dorsey Wakes Up Every Morning at 5:00 AM," *The Hustle*, December 22, 2015.

113. Daniel Pink, *Drive: The Surprising Truth about What Motivates Us* (Canongate Books Ltd, 2011).

114. Liesl Nielsen, "Oprah Tells Utah Audience That 'Your Legacy Is Every Life You Touch,'" KSL.com, 2019, https://www.ksl.com/article/46506476/oprah-tells-utah-audience-that-your-legacy-is-every-life-you-touch.

115. Tom Rath and Gallup Press, *Strengths Based Leadership: Great Leaders, Teams, and Why People Follow* (Gallup Press, 2016).

116. Justin Mackay, "Employee Engagement Survey Overview," Primary Colour Surveys, 2014, https://www.edgecumbe.co.uk/engagement-surveys/.

117. Strategy&, *What drives a company's success? Highlights of survey findings* (PwC, 2013) https://www.strategyand.pwc.com/gx/en/reports/strategyand-what-drives-a-companys-success.pdf.

118. Harvard Business Review, "When Hiring Execs, Context Matters Most," *Harvard Business Review*, September-October 2017, https://hbr.org/2017/09/when-hiring-execs-context-matters-most.

119. Marcel Schwantes, "Bill Gates, Steve Jobs, and Warren Buffett All Agree: These 3 Hiring Strategies Will Land You the Best People," *Inc.*, February 11, 2019, https://www.inc.com/marcel-schwantes/bill-gates-steve-jobs-agree-these-2-brilliant-hiring-strategies-will-land-you-best-people.html.

120. Georg Vielmetter and Yvonne Sell, *Leadership 2030: The Six Megatrends You Need to Understand to Lead Your Company into the Future* (AMACOM, 2014).

121. Ronald F. Inglehart, *Cultural Evolution: People's Motivations Are Changing, and Reshaping the World* (Cambridge University Press, 2018).

122. Laurence Butet-Roch, "Pictures Reveal the Isolated Lives of Japan's Social Recluses," *National Geographic*, February 14, 2018.

123. Michael Zielenziger, *Shutting Out The Sun: How Japan Created Its Own Lost Generation* (Ballantine Books Inc., 2007).

The authors of *The Leader's Secret Code*.
From left to right: Mark Ridley, Ian
Mills, Ben Laker and Adam Pacifico.